WHO WE ARE

WHO WE ARE

A CITIZEN'S MANIFESTO

RUDYARD GRIFFITHS

Douglas & McIntyre

D&M PUBLISHERS INC.
VANCOUVER/TORONTO

Douglas & McIntyre
A division of D&M Publishers Inc.
2323 Quebec Street, Suite 201
Vancouver BC Canada V5T 4S7
www.dmpibooks.com

Library and Archives Canada Cataloguing in Publication
Griffiths, Rudyard
Who we are : a citizen's manifesto / Rudyard Griffiths.

ISBN 978-1-55365-124-6

1. National characteristics, Canadian. 2. Canada—Social
conditions—21st century. 3. Canada—Economic conditions—21st century.
4. Canada—Politics and government—21st century. I. Title.
FC97.G74 2009   971   C2008-907598-6

Jacket design by Naomi MacDougall
Text design and typesetting by Ingrid Paulson
Printed and bound in Canada by Friesens
Printed on acid-free paper that is forest friendly (100% post-consumer recycled paper)
and has been processed chlorine free

We gratefully acknowledge the financial support of the Canada Council for the Arts,
the British Columbia Arts Council, the Province of British Columbia through
the Book Publishing Tax Credit and the Government of Canada through
the Book Publishing Industry Development Program (BPIDP) for our publishing activities.

This book is dedicated to my grandfather,
Group Captain John Francis Griffiths, DFC
July 21, 1905–May 9, 1945

CONTENTS

| INTRODUCTION

ALONG with many Canadians in their thirties, my political coming of age did not coincide with the tumultuous 1988 free-trade election, the failures of the Meech Lake or Charlottetown accords or the fall of the Berlin Wall. These events, momentous as they were, seemed driven by the politics and personalities of my parents' era. The crisis that shook me out of the comfortable "What, me worry?" complacency of adolescence and taught my generation an object lesson in why politics matter was the 1995 Quebec referendum.

The nail-biting drama that unfolded on television screens across the country on that late October evening and the emotional living-room debates that accompanied it seared into my consciousness the precariousness of this project we call Canada. Despite the history we might share or the values we might believe unite us as Canadians, during those anxiety-filled hours the country's continuing existence was measured in mere fractions of a percentage point—a surreal, if not sad, calculation of the sum of our nationhood.

In the aftermath of the referendum and in light of the razor-thin victory eked out by the "No" side, two friends and I decided to do something. To bottle up and ignore the passion that had filled and fuelled the weeks leading up to the final vote seemed to us a capitulation to the very phenomenon that had landed the country in such a mess in the first place, namely our indifference to the common history, enduring values and civic traditions that bind Canadians together, French and English, Aboriginal and immigrant.

Without a scintilla of experience or two sous to rub together, Michael Chong, Erik Penz and I, all in our mid-twenties and freshly out of university, set about the work of launching the Dominion Institute. Our goal was to create an organization that would show Canadians that the country's continued existence should not be presented primarily as an economic proposition or necessity, as so many business and political leaders had argued in the run-up to the referendum. Rather, the Institute would advance the idea that the foundations of our unity should rest, first and foremost, on a deep appreciation and knowledge of the country's past, its enduring civic traditions and the struggles of previous generations to forge an inspiring civic identity capable of bridging our ethnic, regional and linguistic differences in common purpose.

This lofty vision survived to see the light of day thanks to the financial and moral support that followed the official launch of the Institute on Canada Day 1997, when we released the first of many polls that revealed how little Canadians know about their country's history. Our initial splash in the media and a two-year grant from the Donner Canadian Foundation saw the Institute through a challenging start-up period of missed payrolls, bounced rent cheques and a professional staff of only two, myself included. But sure enough, our message about the importance of Canadian history and shared citizenship to the country's future won adherents, and the "DI" became a going concern.

Leading the Institute was an exercise in guerrilla-style public advocacy. We put Louis Riel on trial on the CBC and drew three-quarters of a million viewers in Quebec and English Canada and a raft of Métis protesters. We launched a veterans' speakers' bureau that has helped some 3,000 servicemen and women share their life experiences with upwards of a million school children. We used the media shamelessly (for a decade, the Institute generated, on average, a news story a day) to get our message out. We published books, produced television documentaries and text messaging campaigns, invested in feature films and commissioned a steady stream of public opinion polls. By the time I stepped down as full-time executive director in 2008, we had raised close to $20 million in support of our mandate, employed dozens of committed young people and created a network of 3,700 volunteers who continue to champion the cause of civic literacy in schools and local communities nationwide.

In short, the Institute succeeded beyond our wildest expectations. It redeemed our faith in the relevance of Canada's past and civic traditions to the country's future and restored our conviction that the ties that bind us together are stronger than the forces that would pull us apart.

Our sense of accomplishment aside, when I finally handed over the reins of the Institute I could not help feeling that I was leaving a job half finished. I felt this way because during my final years at the Institute we found ourselves coming up more and more frequently against a view of the country's nature and purpose that was very different from the pan-Canadian philosophy we espoused.

Whether it was our advocacy for more and better history and civics education in the schools or our belief in the centrality of Canada's bicultural foundations to present-day debates about the country's values and institutions, our detractors—within government, academia and some media—took issue with our most basic premises. These critics, many of whom held positions of influence and power, openly questioned the merits of maintaining, let alone nurturing, a strong national identity based on shared institutions, deeply felt social obligations and widely held civic values.

At conferences, in books and op-ed pieces and through their own advocacy groups, our antagonists contended that Canada had entered a new phase in its development, a period in which the multiple loyalties and strong regional identities that have always been constants in Canada—French vs. English, Central Canada vs. the West and Atlantic Canada, for example—were being accentuated by the effects of globalization, within and beyond our borders. As a result, the work of the Institute and similar groups to promote a common Canadian identity supposedly risked unsettling the uneasy peace between the country's regions, its historic minority groups and its national government and institutions. According to this line of reasoning, the Institute's efforts to assert a common civic creed in our schools and popular culture also threaten the fuzzy and indeterminate nature of what it means to be Canadian today, the much-vaunted national trait that allegedly allows us to thrive as a country comprised of disparate regions, peoples and groups who embrace a myriad of allegiances, ancestries and far-flung homelands. These are not just the views of an academic fringe. One in three Canadians surveyed by the Institute in a nationwide poll in 2007 stated that part of what makes Canada a successful society is "the *lack* of a strong national identity that individuals and groups are expected to adopt."

This view, repeated over and over on issue after issue, convinced me that although we like to joke that the only thing Canadians can agree on is that we are "not Americans," growing numbers of our fellow citizens have embraced concepts and purposes for the country that are fundamentally different from the long-held assumptions of previous generations—assumptions that our forebears thought were essential to how and why Canada works.

These notions and the lesson of the 1995 referendum—a reminder of how tenuous our loyalties to each other as Canadians can become if the enduring beliefs and principles we share as a people are not forcefully posited and promulgated—compelled me to put pen to paper and write this book.

I wanted to take on the now commonplace assertion that Canada is, and has always been, a nation shaped by regions and comprised of ethnic and linguistic groups who define themselves as different and who wish to remain so. This was not what I felt when I travelled the country for the Institute and worked with people and organizations who believe ardently in the relevance of the institutions, symbols and memory of a common nationhood. The notion that each of us is a concoction of "multiple identities" and that whatever collective vision we have for our country should be conditioned by this fact seemed to me out of step with Canadians' desire to be part of a shared civic enterprise, an enterprise that has roots stretching back more than four centuries and that encompasses, at this moment in our history, everything from our efforts to bring stability to war-ravaged Afghanistan to our experiment with the world's highest levels of legal per capita immigration to battling the effects of climate change across a national land mass second only to Russia's.

I believe that the view that Canadians are, and always have been, a people defined by the multiplicity of their loyalties is based on a highly self-serving and comparatively recent reinterpretation of our history. As this book asserts, well before the patriation of the Constitution and the advent of the Charter of Rights and Freedoms, Canadians already had a clear understanding about who we were as a people and what we had set out to accomplish together. Our founding principles and core beliefs gelled during two great imaginings of Canada. The first of these occurred in the decade that followed the failed rebellions in Upper and Lower

Canada, between 1838 and 1848. In the face of deep sectarian divisions that regularly boiled over into mayhem and murder, and opposed by colonial governments prepared to use the full power of the state to quash any challenge to their authority, French and English reformers banded together to create the civic institutions and values that made democratic self-government in Canada a reality. This singular accomplishment, achieved during a period of great social and economic tumult, forged an enduring consensus as to whom Canadians should be loyal to and why.

Canada's second great imagining of itself occurred not at Confederation, Vimy Ridge or Expo 67, but at the mid-mark of the twentieth century. United by the experience of fighting and winning the Second World War, and led by a remarkable group of politicians and civil servants, Canadians in the 1950s returned to the principled nation building their forebears had initiated a century earlier. Just as in the late 1840s and the 1850s, our institutions and national symbols were renewed and rethought to reflect Canadians' commitment to a common civic enterprise that was neither British nor American, but something uniquely our own.

The core tenet that links these two remarkable decades, a century apart, is our forebears' belief that, above all else, Canadians must remain loyal to themselves—that our highest duty as a people is to build institutions and inculcate values that unite us around a shared vision for our society, one that reflects the historical and social realities of our nation, Canada. Elucidating the principles and beliefs that arose during these two seminal periods and resisting the country's current slide into an ornery amalgam of regional statelets and grievance-riven minorities is the pressing issue of our time and the intent of this book.

It's the pressing issue facing us today because, according to a host of indicators, Canada's relative isolation from the churn of global events is fast coming to an end. Whether it is dealing with the planet-wide causes and effects of climate change or the ticking demographic time bomb that threatens the social and financial well-being of our population, it is a matter of when, not if, we will be ejected from our comfy redoubt atop North America to face a new set of challenges to our collective way of life.

Once Canada is well and properly ensnared by one of these existential threats, the country will necessarily face the kind of test that our forebears confronted in the 1840s and in the middle of the last century and that we almost failed on that late October evening in 1995.

The question we have to ask ourselves is whether we have the requisite levels of social solidarity to endure a prolonged national crisis that severely strains the country's institutions and our loyalty to each other. Is there enough trust and shared knowledge among Canadians today to maintain the kind of broad social consensus that experience tells us is essential to coping with the major challenges the country could face in its near future?

It is my contention that in the next decade or two Canadians will have to rely as never before in our recent history on reserves of cultural capital—the common institutions, symbols, values and beliefs that define our shared nationhood—that were created and husbanded by past generations. We will have to rediscover, and quickly, what we have in common rather than fixating on our differences and hiving ourselves off from each other on the basis of language, region and ethnicity. In effect, we must return to an older and more substantive national conversation about what it means to be Canadian, a conversation in which we reimagine for our own time, in clear and precise terms, who we are.

Anticipating what this third great imagining of Canada could embrace is the thread that runs through this book. And on that score I am optimistic about our prospects. There are too many parallels between the challenges facing Canada today and the issues and debates that stimulated the country's earlier great imaginings to deny that our past can be the guide to our future. Figuring out how to reawaken Canadians' sense of civic duty or make our national institutions and symbols relevant to young people or use our shared citizenship to give newcomers and the long-settled a sense of common purpose—these are all questions that our forebears wrestled with and worked through as they imagined and reimagined their country.

Rediscovering this treasure trove of insights into how and why the country works is more than just an intellectual exercise for historians and policy wonks. We have a responsibility beyond doing right by the generations of Canadians who propelled our country from colony to nation-state. Our collective task is to ensure that the ambitious civic project our society set for itself more than a century and a half ago—to reconcile our differences in a single and compelling vision of Canadian nationhood—continues, whatever an increasingly uncertain world throws our way.

In this spirit, and with this objective in mind, let's begin.

1 | NATION OR NOTION?

ON the afternoon of November 22, 2006, the House of Commons set about the people's business with predictable acrimony. This was the second minority Parliament in three short years, and during question period, income trusts, health care and equalization payments were debated with the obligatory finger pointing and heckling as the parties vied with each other for the coveted ten-second clip on the evening news.

Following those raucous exchanges, just as the members settled down to the routine tabling of bills and reports, Prime Minister Stephen Harper rose to his feet. Sober and business-like, he informed the House that his government would, later that afternoon, formally introduce a motion of vital national importance. The chamber fell quiet.

Invoking visionaries of the past—"When Champlain landed in Quebec, he did not say that this would not work, it was too far away, it was too cold, or it was too difficult…Champlain and his companions worked hard…to build a lasting and secure country"—the prime minister signaled the historic significance of his motion, a bold proposal that his caucus had learned about only that morning and that every parliamentarian would be called to vote on within a matter of days.

Throughout his eight-minute address, he was repeatedly interrupted by spontaneous applause, not only from his cabinet and Conservative backbenchers but from Liberals and New Democrats, too. It was an extraordinary outburst of collegiality in a legislative session that had been relentlessly combative even by Ottawa standards. Energized by the response, the prime minister ended his statement with a stirring declaration: "To millions...who live in a dangerous and dividing world, this country is a shining example of the harmony and unity [of] which all peoples are capable and to which all humanity should aspire."

Next to rise was the interim leader of Her Majesty's Loyal Opposition, the patrician Bill Graham, who began his remarks by acknowledging that the warm reception accorded the prime minister's words "clearly indicates the devotion of all federalist members in this House to the cause, first and foremost, of Canada, beyond all partisan purposes." Graham, too, seemed caught up in the spirit of his call to action and the buoyant mood of the House. Echoing Harper's sentiments, Graham proclaimed to the assembled legislators that "People are looking for examples in a modern world that will give them hope. It is the duty of the members of this House to give them that hope."

His words, too, were greeted with loud applause and desk thumping on both sides of the House, as the three federalist parties now competed with each other to demonstrate their unreserved support for Graham's statement. Riding the applause, Graham ended with a flourish: "There are many people who wish to move into a peaceful and socially harmonious 21st century and for whom Canada will remain a beacon...We cannot let them down and we must not let ourselves down...We will be faithful to our country, to our principles and...we will be faithful to humanity."

Then, as if on cue, the prime minister jumped to his feet and strode across the floor of the House of Commons, his hand outstretched to the leader of the opposition. Surrounded by standing and clapping Liberal MPs, the two men, mortal ideological enemies, shook hands and embraced across Graham's desk. This extraordinary image of political common cause was flashed on television screens that evening and reproduced on front pages the following day.

Canada's parliamentarians had not come to an agreement about Canada's future role in Afghanistan, where forty-three of their fellow citizens had been killed by that date and where Canada was making its largest military commitment since the Korean War. Nor, despite the soaring metaphors about the country being a beacon of hope in a dangerous world, had our elected representatives at last committed Canada to its long-standing goal of contributing 0.7 percent of its GDP to foreign aid. Their show of solidarity in Parliament that day was likewise not inspired by the country's leaders summoning the will to address our cash-starved cities, strained immigration system or endemic Aboriginal poverty. Instead, what united the country's federal political parties in this fractious and divided legislature was a motion to recognize that "the Québécois form a nation within a united Canada."

The parliamentary lovefest was short-lived, of course; like much else in that chamber, it was the child of self-interest and survival. For the prime minister, the government's motion was a strategic upstaging of an earlier proposal by the separatist Bloc Québécois to acknowledge Quebec—the political entity—as a nation, full stop. That motion threatened to divide the Quebec members of the prime minister's caucus from the rest of the Conservative Party, and so a more palatable alternative had been fashioned. Given the Conservatives' gains in Quebec in the previous federal election, the first significant gains since Brian Mulroney's back-to-back majority victories in 1984 and 1988, the symbolism of acknowledging that the Québécois—as a people—constituted a "nation" within Canada would not be lost on Quebec voters.

For the fratricidal Liberals, the prime minister's motion was a godsend. They were just days away from a national leadership convention in Montreal where the issue of whether or not to recognize the Québécois as a nation threatened to shipwreck the party of Pierre Elliott Trudeau. Speedy passage of the government's motion would eliminate that item from the convention agenda and head off a potential donnybrook in the halls and hospitality suites of the Palais des congrès.

In the wider political world, too, there was a sense among the country's elites that formal recognition of the Québécois as a nation, however hazily defined, was a harmless gesture, if not an overdue acknowledgment of a sociological fact. After all, Quebec's laws, language and institutions had been recognized and protected in various forms for over two centuries. In its recent history, the province had established an old-age pension plan, had acquired extensive powers over immigration and had adopted its own Charter of Rights and Freedoms. It operated a Quebec Department of International Affairs with twenty-six offices abroad and in 2006 was given by the federal government its own seat on the Canadian delegation to the United Nation's cultural body, UNESCO. The government of Quebec also enjoyed a growing and formal role in global climate-change talks. If bestowing the label "nation" on the people of Quebec stymied separatists while assuaging soft nationalists, then the motion was, according to conventional wisdom, smart politics. It affirmed a long-standing tradition of accepting the province's uniqueness, but did so without invoking the spectre of constitutional change. Commenting on his motion to the media, Stephen Harper declared: "We're proud of it...It's inextricably linked to our history, to our status as a bilingual and great country."

Outside of Parliament's hallowed halls, initial reaction from the media and the pundits was largely positive, at times verging on fawning. Most of the news coverage focussed on the immediate political context, praising the prime minister for outfoxing the Bloc and masterfully handling both his own caucus and the Liberals. A number of commentators welcomed the move as a sign of Canada's growing maturity as a nation. To the *Globe and Mail's* John Ibbitson, a shrewd observer of national politics, the motion was a welcome breath of fresh air: "For anyone under 40, it's so obvious that Quebec is its own nation that the subject isn't worth discussing. They know what matters far more is the progress of the Quebec nation and the evolving post-national Canada to which it belongs as we continue the adventure of shaping the world's first truly multicultural state."

In other words, the motion represented a much-needed system update, but not a full-scale reboot, of the country's operating code. The thinking was that the motion would acknowledge not only Quebec's distinctiveness in a non-constitutional fashion, but also the positive changes Canada itself had experienced since the wrenching failures at Meech Lake and Charlottetown. The country had progressed. As a result of Canada becoming more diverse in the closing decades of the twentieth century, Canadians were no longer reluctant, in the first decade of the twenty-first century, to formally recognize the Québécois or any other historic minority group as "national" communities with their own histories and cultures. Various Aboriginal rights were already formally recognized in the Constitution and official multiculturalism implicitly acknowledged that we were a country made up of not one, but many identities. In the view of observers like John Ibbitson, opponents of the motion—all those fogies forty years of age and older who were still wistful about Expo 67 and Trudeaumania—failed to appreciate the degree to which the country had left behind a one-size-fits-all identity and was fast becoming a postnational community of multiple cultures if not multiple "nations."

Alongside those who supported the motion on cultural grounds was an influential group that embraced it for ideological reasons. For a small but influential group of western Conservatives and soft nationalists in Quebec—the two groups that constituted Stephen Harper's powerbase within his party—the Québécois-as-nation debate came down to an argument about the nature of federalism and the purpose of central government in Canada. They favoured the motion as an important step in the creation of the more "open federalism" that had become Conservative Party policy during the previous election. The government's clearly stated objective was to give the provinces a greater say in the creation and delivery of jointly funded programs and, in the name of efficiency and effectiveness, to remove the federal government from a number of areas of provincial jurisdiction altogether. In the words of the prime minister, "[Ottawa's] spending power has created a dominating federalism, a paternalist federalism, which seriously threatens the future of our federation."

Rather than being the agents of a positive pan-Canadian identity, said these Conservatives, the federal government and its institutions more often than not exacerbated the country's unity problems vis-à-vis Quebec and fomented regional alienation in Western and Atlantic Canada. In this context, the motion was viewed as another sign of the prime minister's intention to deal with the regions in a manner very different from the supposedly centralizing and power-obsessed federal governments of the past. Influential Calgary-based commentator Barry Cooper predicted: "When the declaration that the Québécois form a nation...is followed [by] the restoration of the constitutionally proper balance between Ottawa and the several provinces, the Quebec problem will vanish." According to this analysis, to oppose the motion on the grounds that it weakened Canadian unity was misguided, a throwback to the Trudeau era when the federal government assumed that its interests were synonymous with the nation's. In fact, the ideologues argued, the motion was a principled rebalancing of Canadian federalism. It signaled that Ottawa was finally recognizing the decentralized reality of Canada, relinquishing to the provinces their historic powers and the ability to shape their own futures and, by default, that of the country as a whole.

On reflection, it is understandable that public debate about whether or not the Québécois should be officially regarded as a national group within Canada was muted in comparison to the controversy aroused just two decades earlier by the prospect of recognizing Quebec as a "distinct society." By 2006, if you opposed the nation motion you were either being churlish about the role of the Québécois in Confederation or insensitive to the multicultural and postnational ethos of twenty-first-century Canada. Or you were naive about the role national governments could hope to play in Canadians' lives. In sum, the smart money was behind the motion. The political upside in Quebec was simply too advantageous to resist and the downside for the rest of the country seemed somewhere between negligible and nil.

A NEW NORTHERN NATION

From my post at the Dominion Institute, I took a different view of the events in Ottawa and the ensuing debate. I saw the government's motion as a litmus test of sorts, both for my organization and for the country as a whole. Over the previous decade, the Institute had invested in an all-out campaign to remind Canadians of the political traditions and beliefs that had given rise to a common civic identity in Canada. Our contention was, and is, that the country's greatness rests on overcoming divisions of race, language and religion by building institutions and reinforcing values that allow each of us, as citizens possessing equal rights and responsibilities, to pursue an ideal of the common good.

Some of these shared values are immediately familiar to us and passionately embraced, such as religious tolerance or the constellation of principles embodied in the Charter of Rights and Freedoms. Other accomplishments, such as the achievement of responsible government in the 1840s or the creation of our first universal social programs after the Second World War, are fading from our collective memory. But, together with numerous other milestones in our past, they constitute a discernible trajectory of our evolution as a nation-state: an enduring impulse to build a democracy where equal and autonomous individuals come together to chart their collective future.

Certainly, the country has experienced setbacks in its journey from a gaggle of colonies divided internally along sectarian lines to a modern nation-state. Being Canadian means we are all too familiar with our myriad failures, from the expulsion of the Acadians to the near breakup of the country at the time of the 1995 Quebec referendum. But in spite of our disappointments, we are a people who have laboured, over generations, to advance the idea that our deepest attachments and obligations should be to a common civic identity, to a form of nationhood that, while imperfect, strives to transcend our ethnic, regional and linguistic differences with an inspiring and undifferentiated citizenship. The challenge that has long stood before us as a people and to which we have risen time and time again was stated best by a father of Confederation, Thomas D'Arcy McGee: "to lift ourselves to the level of our destinies, to rise above all low limitations and narrow circumscriptions, to cultivate that true catholicity of spirit which embraces all creeds, all classes, and all races, in order to make...a great new northern nation."

The intention of Canada's Parliament to recognize the Québécois as a nation within a united Canada and the reaction that followed was, for me, less about formalizing Quebec's growing autonomy or undermining the separatist cause than it was about the sorry state of Canadian nationhood. I found it incredible that so many leading academics and political commentators believed that this motion was a simple matter of confirming the obvious. The indifference of the country's elites to what was in effect a fundamental recasting of the ideals of Canadian nationhood seems to me to stem from a pervasive sense of exhaustion with the work of nation building. Journalist Andrew Coyne correctly excoriated the political class for its apathy: "We have learned to habituate ourselves to impotence and inertia, to snicker at the grandiloquent boasts of our ancestors...[this motion] marks the moment when the idea of Canada finally shrugged, sighed, heaved and expired."

Those of us who opposed the motion did so in part because recognizing the nationhood of the Québécois—traditionally defined by their shared history, language and geography—seemed to open the door to the emergence of an ethnic nationalism in *la belle province* that might, or might not, be tolerant of the rights of the Aboriginal population, of anglophones and of the 40,000 immigrants who settle in Quebec every year. But our larger objection was to the fact that the motion renounced, seemingly for reasons of political expedience, the country's 140-year-old drive to overcome its existential dilemma, what Lord Durham diagnosed in his famous 1839 report as "two nations warring in the bosom of a single state...a struggle, not of principles, but of races."

And historically, overcome we did. Whether it was the alliance of French and English reformers who fought to bring democracy to the colonies in 1848, or the bicultural partnership that achieved

Confederation in 1867, or the sacrifices of 5,000 or more Canadian francophones who died in the service of their country in two world wars, the most ennobling work of our nation has been to join the different cultures that emerged out of two of history's great empires in a single civic enterprise.

Yes, the motion was simply symbolic as its supporters claimed—but symbols matter. They are the touchstones of countries and peoples, especially so for a nation that is founded on an idea rather than on a common racial or linguistic heritage. By dismissing the motion as insignificant, the country's intellectual elites and much of the media revealed their profound misunderstanding of, or sheer indifference to, the country's history and Canada's overarching purpose.

Those who supported the motion on the grounds that it acknowledged the decentralized reality of present-day Canada at least did so with some rationale. It has not been easy at the best of times, let alone in the wake of the sponsorship scandal, to make a case that the federal government is a wellspring of national cohesion or shrewd financial oversight, particularly in Quebec. Also, who is to say that a bureaucrat or politician in far-off Ottawa understands the needs of local communities better than their provincial counterparts who often live and work in the very areas where government policy is trying to make a difference? In our ever more interconnected world, it often falls to local communities to shoulder the burden of social change, to deal with environmental, financial and demographic issues that were traditionally the purview of national institutions and central governments.

The problem with this rationale is that it ignores the fact that Canada is not like most countries. In a whole host of ways we are the exception, not the norm. First, we are already one of the most economically decentralized federations in the world. According to the Centre for the Study of Democracy at Queen's University, the federal government's share of tax revenues raised by both levels of government in Canada in recent years is a paltry 40-odd percent. This compares with a 69 percent federal share in Australia and a 67 percent federal share in the United States. Second, we are geographically decentralized to an extraordinary degree. Over 80 percent of Canadians live within a narrow corridor measuring 150 kilometers deep and 5,000 kilometers wide, perched on top of the Canada–U.S. border. Add to these structural challenges two major language groups, strong north-south economic currents, rapid urbanization and the world's only superpower next door, and you have a body politic whose sinews are inherently stretched. In the short term it may well transpire that an agenda of "open federalism," including the recognition of the Québécois as a nation and the limiting of federal spending powers, will buy peace with the provinces and better define the role of the federal government in domestic matters. But it is far from certain that the further decentralization of our federation will strengthen the Canadian nation over the long term.

Dealing with the major challenges Canadians could soon face—global warming, mass immigration and a fast-aging population, to name three that will be examined in detail here—may very well require a substantial reassertion of federal power. Having, say, ten divergent job-training programs, climate-change strategies or immigration systems, all with their own priorities, could prove a recipe for disaster when confronting problems that respect no borders and require national and global coordination. So, too, could the loss of a single voice for Canada on the world stage when the interests of the Québécois "nation" conflict with those of the rest of the country in international forums or when Alberta decides to use its growing network of trade and policy offices abroad to facilitate access to the province's natural resources in exchange for preferential treatment of its exports. As well-intentioned as ideological decentralists might be in wanting to strengthen their country, the doctrine of open federalism and the recognition of Québécois nationhood could ultimately undermine Canadians' interests at home and abroad.

This brings me to the one argument in favour of the motion that made me question my own beliefs about Canada. What if the country is truly in the process of becoming a "postnational" state where our individual needs and expectations of community have changed fundamentally? What if recognizing the Québécois as a nation signals the entrenchment of a new, laissez-faire understanding of Canadian citizenship? What if it represents simply the latest step in our transformation into a country of not one but many "nations"— the Québécois "nation," Aboriginal "nations," Métis "nation," the Acadian "nation" and "nations" of other minority groups?

Thinkers such as historian Michael Bliss objected strongly to such presumptions. Bliss opposed the motion because with its passage we would have "members of the Quebec nation—a nation within a nation—and we [would] have the rest of Canada. The premier of Quebec is the head of a nation...The provinces are no longer equal. Canadians are no longer equal." Put another way, the premiers of Quebec could claim, within Canada and on the world stage, that they represented the interests of a full-blown "nation" and thereby demand a higher order of recognition from other "nations," a process that is well underway with Quebec having attained its own quasi-official standing in global climate-change talks, its own seat at UNESCO and a Quebec-only labour mobility agreement with the government of France. In essence, the motion created two tiers of citizenship. To a degree completely unprecedented in our history, those living inside Quebec now have a qualitatively different standing vis-à-vis the federal government and a growing list of international bodies and countries than those in the rest of Canada. As constitutional veteran Roy Romanow succinctly put it at the time: "There is no longer a place for a national vision of being Canadian based on national citizenship."

However, these arguments and my own belief in an enduring common civic identity are predicated on the idea that most Canadians still see membership in the Canadian nation as a cornerstone of their individual identities. I would venture that part of the reason why so many among the country's elites reacted to the proposed motion with a collective yawn was that the locus of community in Canada has steadily shifted away from the traditional institutions and symbols of nationhood to new markers of belonging and identity. There are numerous indicators, explored in the coming chapters, that suggest that ethnicity, region and social class are figuring more prominently in how we define ourselves as individuals. If this is the overall trend for our society, then recognizing the Québécois, or any other "national" group for that matter, means far less than it did when Canadian citizenship and a common nationhood were more central to our identities, times such as the immediate postwar period or the centennial year. Put differently, devaluing the currency of our shared citizenship by recognizing a Québécois "nation" is less contentious when there are other sources for the sense of purpose and community that we all seek in our day-to-day lives.

Yet for me personally, giving up the idea of building a single, encompassing civic identity with my fellow citizens from Tuktoyaktuk to Timmins, whether they have been in Canada for four years or four hundred, is to accept a diminished country. In my case, searching for a sense of community and belonging based on my nascent Welsh-Canadian or Ontarian-Canadian sense of identity holds few, if any, personal attractions. State-sponsored leek festivals and John Graves Simcoe Day celebrations seem paltry recompense for the loss of a robust and vital civic enterprise that stretches back more than two centuries, a project where the decisions I make along with my 33 million fellow Canadians matter to the future of our country and the larger world.

Just as important, to embrace a postnational vision of Canada's future is to betray Canada's past. Our predecessors spent a significant part the last two hundred years fighting their way out of the claustrophobic identities of race, region and religion so that we could enjoy what philosopher Michael Sandel calls "a public life of larger meaning." Proponents of a postnational vision of Canada are far too quick to exchange the ambition and perseverance of earlier generations for the personally comfortable but ultimately limited expectations of a country made up of multiple "nations," regional factions and issue-oriented communities.

. . .

After less than a week's public debate, on November 27, 2006, the Parliament of Canada voted 266 to 16 in favour of the motion "that the Québécois form a nation within a united Canada." A majority of the members of each party, including the Bloc Québécois, supported it. Interestingly, a significant portion of MPs who were immigrants or visible minorities voted against the motion. Michael Chong, a co-founder of the Dominion Institute and Conservative MP, courageously resigned from cabinet and abstained from the vote.

For Bloc leader Gilles Duceppe, passage of the motion was a sideways, but nonetheless significant, step towards sovereignty: "Nations have rights, including the right to direct their own development…Canada became the first country to officially recognize, in its democratic structures, Quebec as a nation. One day, many other countries will recognize the nation of Quebec and Quebec as a country."

Whether the motion furthered Duceppe's dream of a sovereign Quebec or removed a long-standing irritant in Quebecers' relations with the rest of the country, only time will tell. Early indications are not positive. The subsequent push by the Parti Québécois to enact a Quebec citizenship law requiring newcomers to the province to pass a language test and exam on Québécois culture before they can hold elected office or petition the National Assembly was a perverse, but nonetheless predictable outcome of the Quebec nationhood motion. After all, if you have been recognized as a nation, then why not have citizenship laws that advance your national interests, including the promotion of a national culture based on the French language and Québécois history, just like any other self-respecting nation-state?

The sole consolation I took away from an otherwise depressing episode for the country was the Canadian public's disdain for the motion. According to public opinion polls at the time, three in four Canadians rejected the premise that the Québécois form a nation within Canada, including almost four in five francophones outside Quebec. Similarly, the motion was not popular with immigrants who saw it for what it was: the creation of a subcategory of Canadian citizenship to which they could not belong. To quote a letter published by the *Globe and Mail* during this period: "The very essence of Canadian citizenship is that it has proved to be capable of expanding with each wave of immigrants. Could my parents have come to Canada and become Québécois? The obvious answer is No."

Call them ungenerous, naive or oblivious to the forces changing the Canadian federation and the larger world, but the majority of Canadians knew what many of the country's political, media and cultural elites seem to have forgotten: that we achieve our greatest promise and potential as a people when we transcend the forces that would divide us and assert a single, equal and inspiring civic identity.

THE GREAT ACQUIESCENCE

Countries make mistakes. Political self-interest, short-term thinking and a poor memory for the lessons of the past periodically
combine to create lousy public policy. Those who remember the
National Energy Program or the Meech Lake Accord know that
this dynamic is a perennial Canadian phenomenon. Nonetheless,
we have taken comfort in the knowledge that whatever damage
we cause to the edifice of Canadian nationhood, the country's
reserves of accommodation and common purpose will soon set
us aright, back on the path of conciliation and progress.

Although I once shared this confidence, recent events have led
me to different conclusions. I would argue that the failure of our
political leaders and opinion makers to rally the country to the
defence of a common nationhood, in name and fact, fits into a larger
pattern of collective acquiescence. Beyond politics, in the areas of
culture, the economy and our social priorities, the country's elites
and institutions are failing to assert the symbols, shared objectives
and values that defined our common identity for our forebears and
continue to do so for much of the Canadian public today.

Take Canadian citizenship, for example. Consider for a moment
the incredible benefits that come with holding a Canadian passport: extraordinary individual freedom, the privilege of living in
a tolerant, peaceful and open society, and some of the world's
most generous cradle-to-grave social programs. Add to that, as
journalist Richard Gwyn put it, the expectation "to be welcomed
abroad, as a representative of a country that...tries to help other
people achieve some of the conditions of democracy, the rule of
law, and respect for human rights." All in all an impressive bundle
of privileges and constitutional rights.

Yet our citizenship laws suggest that the good fortune to be
able to call Canada home has become an afterthought for succes-

sive federal governments and more and more of our "fellow" citizens. It is not simply that, among Western nations, we have some of the least onerous residency requirements for newcomers or that we continue to sell our citizenship to investor class immigrants for a paltry $100,000. It is how we have steadily chipped away at the few rights and privileges that resident citizens of Canada enjoy as compared with the more than 2.5 million Canadian citizens who choose to live abroad, many permanently. This group pays little or no taxes and is not expected to contribute in any substantive way to the betterment of the country to which they belong. Yet after six months of residency, they enjoy access to the health care system and to heavily subsidized post-secondary education. And, in the case of the 2006 Lebanon War, thousands of Canadian citizens who had never set foot in Canada could expect the federal government to violate the territorial sovereignty of another state (the Canadian chartered ships that undertook the "rescue" docked in Beirut without the permission of the Lebanese government) and evacuate them at the cost of $94 million or some $6,000 per person.

The slew of benefits conferred on these citizens of convenience needs to be juxtaposed to the struggles of newcomers who choose to put down roots in Canada, undertake to master a new language, climb a steep economic ladder and pay taxes, yet receive few additional considerations for making the country their permanent home. This cavalier disregard for the institution of Canadian citizenship is exhibited in a period when the advantages of being a Canadian citizen are arguably greater than at any time in our recent past. The reality is that Canadians today enjoy a reassuring geographic distance from the globe's trouble spots, an absence of civil strife and an abundance of resources in a world clamouring for clean air and water. By any measure Canada is a pretty good place to call home for the foreseeable future.

One might expect therefore that our governments and national institutions would recognize this and ask its citizens—especially those lucky enough to be born in the country—to assume some of the obligations of citizenship, such as mandatory voting or national service, that other Western nations, such as Australia, Denmark, Switzerland and Germany, regard as essential to the smooth functioning of their societies. But no—whether you are a newcomer to the country or your family has been in Canada for generations, there are few substantive responsibilities associated with belonging to one of world's great democracies. We tolerate turnout rates in federal elections of less than two-thirds of eligible voters and less than a quarter of first-time voters. Similarly, although we are quick to describe ourselves as a caring society, only a small percentage of us are responsible for most formal volunteer work and civic-minded activity, such as joining community associations, attending a political rally or writing to a Member of Parliament. Not only are the duties of citizenship almost ethereal, but the lack of meaningful civic commitment and engagement suggests many of us have a deep-seated apathy towards the very kinds of democratic values and practices that previous generations thought were fundamental to sustaining our collective way of life.

Linked to this diluted version of citizenship is the short shrift given to the teaching of Canadian history and civics in our schools. The failure to convey to the next generation the stories of their forebears comes with a heavy price. In the words of historian Desmond Morton, "People who lose their history, as the First Nations know better than anyone, lose their place... They are victims of robbery without hope of redress." Incredible as it seems in a country so concerned with its cultural sovereignty, only three of ten provinces require students to take a course in twentieth-century Canadian history before graduating from high school. In the majority of our school systems, history is taught, if at all, as "social studies," accurately described by historian Jack Granatstein as "a mishmash of civics, pop sociology and English as a second language, eliminating anything that might offend students, parents, and school trustees, in an attempt to produce an air-brushed past free of warts." The result of neglecting to teach history, government, political systems and the rights and duties of citizenship is a growing civic literacy crisis that has profound implications for our democracy.

In 2007, a national survey conducted by the Dominion Institute found that only one in four Canadians aged eighteen to twenty-four—the graduates of some of the world's best-funded public school systems—could identify the date of Confederation. Less than half could name John A. Macdonald as our first prime minister. If the Old Chieftain had known about these dismal findings, he would have at least found solace in the fact that barely one in four young adults was familiar with his arch nemesis, Louis Riel. When compared with an identical twenty-question survey conducted a decade earlier, the 2007 scores indicated that young people's knowledge of some of the major touchstones in our past—Macdonald, Confederation and Riel—had declined, on average, a percentage point a year. These results mirrored other studies the Institute conducted, which showed that already low levels of knowledge of the basic tenets of our democracy have fallen precipitously over the last decade.

For a society as diverse and decentralized as Canada today, civic literacy is surely the lifeblood of our democracy. Ensuring that every citizen possesses a working knowledge of the country's history, geography and political institutions is a fundamental responsibility of parents, schools and governments. If our children grow up not knowing what the date 1867 signifies or what responsible government means or how our laws are made, then they lack the tools required to participate effectively in the complex political and cultural debates that will shape their society. Research studies show that people's political efficacy—their voting rate and overall community involvement—correlates directly with their level of civic literacy. In other words, the very people who most need democratic institutions to advance their interests, the poor and undereducated, are the ones most likely to be disempowered by education systems that fail to equip them with basic civic literacy skills. Considering, too, that we have the highest levels of per capita legal immigration in the world, ensuring that every new citizen acquires these skills and this basic knowledge is an essential act of nation building.

Despite everything we know both about the role of history and civics in sustaining a strong national identity and about the social justice implications of failing to impart this knowledge to every young Canadian, we have, for almost an entire generation, done little as a country to re-invigorate and revive the teaching of our past. Fads in teacher training, the exclusive power of the provinces to determine school curricula and the fact that our history is complicated and full of grievances some would rather forget have conspired to ensure that Canada's past remains a foreign country for all but a minority of Canadians.

Our failure to appreciate the value of our shared citizenship and common patrimony, the country's rich history and civic traditions, runs parallel to a disturbingly casual attitude we have towards Canada's economic fundamentals. We know from prestigious publications such as the *Economist* that the economic decentralization of the country has become one of our key competitive disadvantages: "Turf battles and arguments over money make for inefficient government and lack of accountability as politicians would rather finger point than push through needed [economic] reforms."

Let's consider just one of those turf battles. Canada and Bosnia and Herzegovina are the only two Western federal democracies without a national securities regulator. In countries such as the United States, France and Britain, a single authority streamlines the process of foreign direct investment and centralizes the regulatory oversight of publicly traded companies in one national institution, thereby ensuring greater corporate transparency. Each year the absence of a single regulator costs the Canadian economy billions of dollars in lost capital investments that would otherwise be used to erect new factories, develop technologies that make our work-force more efficient, and create thousands of urgently needed new jobs. Bosnia and Herzegovina is still recovering from a vicious civil war and is a barely functioning federal democracy. What is Canada's excuse? In a nutshell, provincial protectionism and little else. Yes, Alberta's securities commission knows more about the complexities of financing an oil company than its counterpart in Quebec, but the real reason both jurisdictions balk at the imposition of a national regulatory scheme has everything do with provincial pride and deep-seated resistance to any federal leadership.

This parochial outlook is also what is responsible for Canada continuing to maintain the highest barriers to internal trade and commerce of any of its G8 competitors. Impeding the free flow of goods and people across our provincial and territorial borders is estimated to cost the Canadian economy as much as $14 billion per year, or the equivalent of our entire defence budget. While Alberta and British Columbia signed a free-trade pact in 2006 and the other provinces have promised to work towards a national labour-mobility agreement, there is no leadership at the federal level to create a true European-style economic union to drive new growth, productivity and East-West trade.

We know that the federal government has the constitutional power to initiate a genuine economic union if it so chooses. Or, at

a minimum, it could cajole the provinces into lowering the barriers to the free flow of workers (in all sectors including health care),
capital and goods and services by linking an ambitious national
program of economic reform to a pledge to address the provinces'
ongoing concerns about the lack of sustainable health care funding and infrastructure spending.

Instead of bold policy-making at the federal level, however,
we have the provinces entering, as if they were sovereign states,
into a patchwork of bilateral trade agreements with each other,
or in the case of Quebec and its labour mobility laws, with
another nation-state, France. Ottawa's response to these unprecedented challenges to its fiscal oversight of the federation has
been to hand $38 billion to the provinces to solve the supposed
"fiscal imbalance" in the 2006 federal budget, with few, if any,
strings attached, and to cut two percentage points off the GST,
thereby reducing the fiscal capacity of the federal government by
a whopping $10 billion annually. As one commentator correctly
surmised, "a common economic space presupposes a common
political space." Given the country's fractured political landscape
and the unwillingness of the national government to assert its
constitutional prerogatives, it is safe to assume that we will not
enjoy the benefits of either any time soon.

Closely aligned with our failure to advance a national economic policy has been the indifference of corporate Canada and
our federal leaders to foreign takeovers of Canadian-owned-and-
built companies. The increase in foreign-led acquisitions is truly
staggering. Earlier this decade there were on average a couple of
hundred takeovers in Canada every year. Only a small proportion
of them were so-called "megadeals"—transactions valued at over
$1 billion. In 2007, just before the onset of the credit and housing
market crises in the United States, takeovers soared to a couple of
hundred in each quarter, with double the number of foreign

acquisitions qualifying as megadeals. The result is that some of Canada's largest companies—household-name corporations such as the Hudson Bay Company, Alcan and MacMillan Bloedel that were nurtured prudently over generations—have fallen out of Canadian control and into foreign hands.

The loss of these homegrown champions, especially global energy and natural resource powerhouses such as Inco and Falcon-bridge, has to be understood in the context of shifts in our economy and in global markets. Canada is no longer producing companies like Nortel or Research In Motion. The successful high-tech enterprises we created in the 1990s when the country was supposedly moving towards a knowledge-based economy were either vaporized when the dotcom bubble burst or, like graphic chip leader ATI Technologies Inc. and software giant Cognos Inc., taken over by larger, primarily American, competitors.

According to Roger Martin, head of the Rotman School of Management, it is conceivable that Canada may soon end up with no "globally relevant consumer electronic company, automotive equipment manufacturer, consumer packaged goods company or beer company...Steel is almost gone and much of mining seems to be headed that way."

Some will argue that the loss of Canadian ownership and control does not necessarily mean shedding jobs or slashing research and development spending in Canada, and that Canadian businesses are acquiring record numbers of companies abroad. While true, these arguments miss the point. Our few remaining corporate heavyweights, especially our large energy and natural resource companies, are the country's best and possibly last hope for maintaining a prominent beachhead in the global economy, a slice of international financial real estate that will accrue the long-term domestic and international advantages that come with being a global leader in a specific sector. These advantages include everything from robust capital markets to global marketing know-how to international transportation hubs, all benefits that will ensure Canada retains its seat at the G8 table and a say in the future evolution of the global economy.

Economists know this, and a few of the country's CEOs, among them Peter Munk, have raised the alarm over the sell-off of Canada's corporate and resource jewels. They point out that the governments of the foreign competitors who are snatching up Canadian firms, such as China, France, Spain and Germany, keep their own energy, finance and resource companies firmly under domestic ownership. In contrast, Canadian governments hem and haw over the merits of making our foreign-ownership regulations for the banking and telecomm sectors even laxer. Or, in the case of our natural resource companies, politicians endlessly fiddle royalty schemes while our shared patrimony—the oil, precious metals and forests whose exploitation built this country—become the property of foreign corporations and governments, among them states that do not share our democratic values or support our international objectives.

In addition to neglecting the economic underpinnings of our federation, we too often miss the opportunities we are given to reinforce important national symbols. The story of First World War veteran Charles Clarence "Clare" Laking is a telling case in point. I first met Charles in 2003 when he was a sprightly 104 years of age. At the time, the Dominion Institute was collecting oral histories from veterans, and with only a handful of Great War survivors still alive, we were eager to record his memories for posterity. Alert, lucid and possessed of a wry sense of humour, he willingly told us the story of his war, how he had enlisted as soon as he turned eighteen and how he spent the following two years trying to cheat death as a signaller on the front lines. He narrowly missed being seriously wounded or worse on more occasions than he could count, and he lost many close friends in battle. Still, he was extremely proud to have been among the all-Canadian forces that were rightly celebrated as liberators in France and Belgium at the war's end.

In every way Charles was an exemplary Canadian, a man who had served his country in war, raised a family, started a business and helped build the country that we live in today. In 2005, he became the last surviving Canadian to have experienced combat in the First World War, the last living link between twenty-first-century Canada and our nation's war of independence—a conflict that cost over 60,000 Canadian lives.

In November 2005, at 106 years of age, Charles Laking passed away peacefully. The previous year Australia had marked the death of their last Great War combat veteran with a full state funeral. Ceremonies were held at local cenotaphs across the country, and the funeral was broadcast on national television. In Canada, officialdom greeted the news of Charles's passing with little more than a perfunctory press release. At the funeral organized by his family, the governments of Britain and France sent official representatives to thank Charles's children and grandchildren for his military service. The country for which Charles and his fellow comrades-in-arms had fought and died sent no one.

The failure to honour Charles Laking's service or to comprehend, as the Australians, British and French clearly did, the larger significance of his death, was a shameful lapse of national character. It is yet another sign of the depth of our neglect of one of the timeless duties of nationhood, namely to honour one's war dead and to ponder, as a people, the awesome responsibilities of citizenship.

. . .

Asserting an inspiring and unifying national identity, upholding not only the rights but also the obligations of citizenship, teaching young people about the country to which they belong, promoting economic prosperity within the country's borders, protecting the sources of its influence in the world and honouring your war dead—these are the pillars of nationhood which have existed since the time of the Greek *polis*. If a country is unable or, in the case of Canada, increasingly unwilling to use the power of the state and its public institutions to advance these ends, then arguably its ability to tackle more complex and intractable issues—skyrocketing health care costs, Aboriginal poverty or regional alienation—becomes suspect.

However, the danger as I see it is not that Canada will break apart because of any single critical issue; nor is it our fate to be subsumed by our more powerful southern neighbour. Canada is too rich, too successful and, increasingly, too important a regional power to be overcome by internal divisions or the siren call of the American empire. Rather, the acquiescence and even entropy that seem to have gripped our elites and many of our institutions could herald an altogether different outcome: inconsequence.

If we continue to slough off our global corporate champions, dilute our citizenship, fail to educate our young about their civic heritage and allow our federation to devolve into ten or more semi-autonomous statelets, Canada will become a shadow of its former self. I fear that if we cannot find our way back to an appreciation of our shared nationhood—its symbols, institutions and common citizenship—we will be transformed, within a generation, into an ornery amalgam of "national" groups and regional fiefdoms, adrift in the backwaters of the global economy and peripheral to the larger trajectory of world events.

2 | THE UNENCUMBERED COUNTRY

SET against the breadth and depth of the Canadian experience—the events, people and places that over four centuries have formed the country—our chronic inability to assert some of the most rudimentary aspects of our shared nationhood and common principles borders on the inexplicable. It is too easy to blame rampant regionalism for the lack of national history and civics instruction in the schools, or to point to laziness and greed for the fire sale of our natural resources. Equally, sloughing off the responsibilities and values of citizenship and ignoring the passing of the last combat veteran of the Great War is the product of more than simple indifference by successive federal governments. I believe we have to look to larger forces to explain the pervasive lassitude among Canadians towards many of the symbols, values and institutions of their nationhood.

Many will recall the "Whither Canada?" debates that raged during a period of economic integration with the United States in the 1970s and 1980s, culminating in the 1988 free-trade election. With every new branch plant that opened, every blockbuster American film that swept into Canadian cinemas or every news story about the brain drain of the country's best and brightest to New York and Los Angeles, Canadians felt that external forces, namely the economic and military might of the United States, were undermining the country's sovereignty and threatening an independent Canadian identity. While these fears later proved to be overstated and the country's sense of itself as a nation culturally distinct from America remained strong in the free-trade era, Canadians had other reasons to be pessimistic about Canada's prospects.

First, the failures of the Meech Lake and Charlottetown constitutional accords produced not only the 1995 Quebec referendum, but also a deep skepticism about Canada's political ruling class and the effectiveness of the country's institutions. Then, in the mid-1990s, Canadians had to endure the pain of drastic federal spending cuts to help rein in the deficits that threatened the country's solvency. The severity of these cuts and the accompanying atmosphere of crisis served to erode Canadians' faith in the national government and its leadership. By the time the country limped into the new century, Prime Minister Jean Chrétien correctly read the country's mood: his minimalist government was as much a conscious choice as it was a reflection of the country's bruised emotional and financial state.

Yet consider what has happened since the late 1990s: Canada has enjoyed some of the highest year-to-year GDP growth of any G8 country, more consecutive federal budget surpluses than any of our G8 competitors and one of the fastest-shrinking debt-to-GDP ratios in the industrialized world—all factors that will help the country weather the current economic downturn.

Global demand for our energy and natural resources has been fuelled by the industrialization of the world's emerging economies, suggesting the forces that contributed to the prosperity of the previous ten years will buoy up the Canadian economy over the long term. We forget that Canada is the world's largest producer of uranium (the zero-greenhouse-gas-emitting energy source that more and more countries are turning to), the second-largest producer of hydroelectric power (another green energy source) and the third- and seventh-place producer respectively of natural gas and oil. Canada is also the steward of the world's second-largest proven hydrocarbon resource: the 173 billion barrels of crude oil locked in Alberta's tar sands. For political scientist John Kirton, "a highly capable Canada has now emerged as a principal power in a rapidly changing world. It is a world defined by a vulnerable America and by a growing demand for, and dependence on, things Canadian from the rising powers...."

On the national unity front, Canadians have witnessed the steady decline of the sovereigntist movement in Quebec. In this regard, the remarkable business acumen of Quebec Inc. has done far more than recognition of the Québécois nation ever could to make Quebeckers feel that they are indeed masters in their own house. The ebbing of the separatist threat is also a reflection of the fact that the French language and Québécois culture are thriving in Quebec while French Canadian artists enjoy international acclaim. More and more Quebeckers, especially young people, sense that the hypothetical rewards of separating from Canada are fast diminishing, whereas the risks—chiefly the economic repercussions—grow with each passing year.

The rest of the country has picked up on Quebec's increasing reconciliation with Canada: in a national poll conducted by the Dominion Institute in 2006, only one in eight hundred respondents surveyed outside of Quebec thought it was "very likely" that the province would separate from Canada by the year 2020.

In the councils of international decision-making, Canada has enjoyed a modest reversal of its decades-long waning influence in world affairs. Thanks to the major contribution we have made to the stabilization of war-torn Afghanistan—our single largest troop deployment since the Korean War—Canada has re-emerged as a key player in NATO. Our status as a large and stable energy exporter has also helped ensure that Canada remains relevant within the G8 at a time when our economic stature is challenged by the growth of the economies of Asia and South America.

The current economic downturn aside, survey after survey shows that Canadians are confident about their country's long-term prospects. We are living through one of those periods in our history filled with significance and potential that in earlier periods gave rise to a surge of nation and legacy building: the achievement of Confederation in the 1860s, our elevation to a leadership role as a senior dominion within the British Empire in the early 1900s, the cultural and infrastructure boom that followed on the heels of the Second World War or the aspirations of Trudeau's "Just Society" in the late 1960s. Yet there is no such assertion of Canadian national ambition on the horizon today. On the contrary, as I have shown, our investment in national projects and institutions is waning, our respect for shared historical and civic traditions evaporating. Why is this happening?

ROOM SERVICE, ANYONE?

In 2002, after he won the Booker Prize for fiction, Canadian novelist Yann Martel was asked to explain why Canadian literature was so popular on the world stage and why his country was producing so many internationally acclaimed authors, such as Rohinton Mistry and Michael Ondaatje, both of whom happen to be immigrants. After praising Canada as a great place for writers to work, Martel made this observation: "It's also the greatest hotel on Earth: it welcomes people from everywhere."

Those five words—"the greatest hotel on Earth"—were seized upon by pundits across the political spectrum as a disheartening and dangerous formulation of Canada's nature and purpose.

Richard Gwyn quipped in the *Toronto Star*: "While it's a lot better to be a five-star hotel than a flophouse, the concept itself is flawed. Hotel guests observe its rules and pay their bills. But that's the extent of their sense of belonging and sense of obligation." Journalist and author Andrew Cohen judged the analogy "perceptive and apt" because "it imagines a Canada in which everyone is a visitor, occupying a room, a floor, or even a wing, depending on his means. No one stays for very long because no one wants to make an extended commitment. A hotel is impermanence, by its very nature the most tenuous of loyalties. People come and go."

In numerous essays and articles since, Martel's country-as-hotel metaphor has been criticized in similar fashion, his more agitated detractors bridling at the notion that Canada is little more than a convenient way station for writer-émigrés to lap up Canada Council grants and then move on when creative whimsy or a more lucrative overseas opportunity beckons. Being Canadian, they assert, is about more than enjoying the freedom to check in and out of "Hotel Canada" with the wave of a Canadian passport at the customs agent-cum-bellhop. It is ultimately about putting down roots and contributing to your local community and the country in meaningful and lasting ways.

In fairness to Martel, his remark was an attempt to explain why Canadian writers were thriving internationally and to make the utterly conventional argument that immigration has enriched the world of Canadian letters. And, he added, Canada is "a good country to write from because in many ways Canada is the world."

However, there is a reason that the concept of Canada as "the greatest hotel on Earth" has taken on a life of its own. Like many writers do, Martel had intuitively but perhaps unconsciously put his finger on the national zeitgeist circa 2002 and the ways Canadians' conversations about the country's goals and purpose were changing. His metaphor gave substance to a new and contentious concept of the country that had been increasingly embraced by our elites, major public and government institutions and a broad section of the media over the previous decade: the notion that the exceptionalism of present-day Canada—what allows us to be simultaneously one of the world's most diverse and harmonious societies—is the indeterminate nature of our national identity.

The rationale behind this fundamental recasting of Canada is that the existence of a common Canadian identity has been disputed since our earliest beginnings. The degrees of attachment that French Canadians, the Aboriginal peoples, religious minorities and regional groups developed for Canada historically were based on the extent to which each group was given the freedom to develop its own sense of community as defined by language, race, faith or geography, rather than being required to root its identity in a common and clearly defined civic culture. To quote philosopher John Ralston Saul, "For centuries we have been making our way from the original complexity of our aboriginal, francophone, anglophone foundations, step by complicated step, to something which is the precise opposite of the Anglo-European-American model of monolithic citizenship."

What is new today is the supposedly happy synchronicity of continuing high levels of immigration and economic globalization with this long-standing but, until recently, latent sense of ourselves as a society of minorities and regions. In a world of transnational identities, free trade and diffused power—all factors that sap the traditional authority of national governments—Canada's lack of a strong national identity, of clearly articulated founding principles or of a broadly shared historical memory are no longer liabilities. Instead, they are purportedly assets when it comes to the smooth functioning of an ever more pluralistic and decentralized society. The absence of a one-size-fits-all national culture creates the opportunity for individuals and groups to define, in their own terms, what it means to be Canadian. The freedom Canada gives to its historic minorities and regions as well as its ethnic and linguistic communities fosters loyalty and attachment, not to the nation of Canada, but to the collective project of tolerating each other's differences and the right to build communities around one's language, region, ethnicity or far-flung homeland.

In the words of globalization enthusiast Pico Iyer, "Canada has become the spiritual home...of the very notion of an extended, emancipating global citizenship," a country quite different from the United States and much of Europe, where nations are still bent on asserting a common identity to which all citizens must subscribe. By adhering to the traditional definition of the nation-state, it is thought, such countries risk courting disaster in a world where aging populations and shrinking workforces must be offset by large numbers of skilled immigrants, individuals who will want to retain their customs and traditions in their adopted country. Similarly, nation-states who resist the empowerment of regions and subnational groups will allegedly exacerbate old secessionist movements and create new and intractable antagonisms between central and outlying governments. In the twenty-first century, successful nations, the argument goes, will be those that relax their rigid definitions of shared nationhood. They will embrace cultural and religious autonomy for newly settled ethnic groups and significantly greater political independence for their regions, just as Canada has done in recent decades. Poet and essayist B.W. Powe sums up this world view best when he celebrates Canada as the country "that accepts and acknowledges pluralism and multiple perspectives...a state whose very lack of a single identity, its lack of homogeneity, is its destiny."

I believe this postnational vision of Canada, now widely touted and warmly embraced in many quarters, is fuelling a sweeping and potentially disastrous realignment of our public institutions, civic values and personal convictions. The prevalence of the view that Canada's weak civic identity is an asset in a globalized world goes a long way towards explaining why we are so reluctant, at this juncture in our history, to affirm a shared vision of Canada's past, to define and celebrate our national symbols and heroes, to demand substantive civic obligations of our citizens and to engage in the kind of nation building that distinguished our journey from colony to nation-state. I believe the reimagining of Canada as a "postnational" state threatens to jettison holus-bolus a set of invaluable understandings about what, in fact, makes our country work: the distilled wisdom and labours of past generations to create a strong and independent Canada.

Those of us who yearn for a fuller and more boldly articulated civic identity need to take the "Hotel Canada" metaphor seriously. Canada and the world are changing, and while the image of the country as a temporary way station for some of its citizens and an undemanding room-service provider for others may be unappealing, it does speak to the increasing tenuousness of our sense of national identity. We are more diverse, more decentralized and ultimately, I suggest, more uncertain about who we are as a people than at any time in our recent history. And, if we are going to find a way back to the core beliefs and first principles upon which the greatness of our country rests, we need to understand the forces and attitudes responsible for the unencumbered state of the Canadian identity.

THE POSTNATIONAL DREAM

The seeds of the "Hotel Canada" vision of the country were planted in the 1970s, the decade when Canadians' attitudes towards government underwent a sea change. Like the citizens of most

Western democracies, we, too, lost confidence in our democratic institutions, government bureaucracies and national forums of all kinds.

According to the much-discussed "decline of deference" thesis— the notion that as societies become more affluent, deference to institutional authority and general community loyalty gives way to a search for personal fulfillment, individual self-esteem and quality of life—the waning interest in traditional forms of political engagement was not unique to the baby-boom generation. It was not a brief rebellious phase born of the late 1960s, one that would pass when the boomers entered middle age and embraced their parents' respect for the authority of government and the processes of formal politics. Rather, first the boomers and then subsequent generations, mine included, have come to view the institutions of the state, party politics and basic civic duties as largely irrelevant to their day-to-day lives, if not as obstacles to their individual self-fulfillment. As social commentator Allan Gregg put it, the 1980s with their economic upheavals, spiralling government deficits, political scandals and constitutional failures "demonstrated all too clearly that the rules that once governed society no longer worked...Paradoxically, discarding the old rules conferred a sense of independence and power on Canadians. They refused, *a priori*, to believe what traditional authorities said, confident that they could make up their own minds."

It is remarkable that in a country with a long history of populist political movements, such as the Women's Christian Temperance Union, the Cooperative Commonwealth Federation and the Social Credit Party, only 16 percent of Canadians today have ever held membership in a political party. This number drops to 5 percent among those thirty years of age and younger, making the average age of members of all political parties in Canada a well-seasoned fifty-nine years.

Our growing disillusionment with political parties has been matched by a steady decline in overall voting rates. In the last quarter century, voter turnout in federal elections has fallen from an average of 74 percent of eligible voters in the 1980s to 66 percent in the 1990s and to below 60 percent in the 2008 election—the lowest recorded turnout ever. The culprits here are first-time voters who are going to the polls in fewer numbers with each successive election. Electoral returns show that fully two-thirds of Canadians who voted for the first time between 1974 and 1980 continued to vote at the same respectable rate in each subsequent election. But for my generation or anyone who reached voting age after 1988, the voting rate is less than one-third. And my peers and I have continued to vote at the same low rate for the last two decades. It seems that not voting, like not taking out membership in a political party or not reading a newspaper, becomes a lifetime habit. With participation rates for first-time voters now tracking as low as 25 percent in some recent federal elections, it is a statistical certainty that national governments will be soon elected by less than half of all eligible voters.

Canadians' disenchantment with political parties and the ballot box is part of the general decline in trust in government, particularly the federal government, and in institutions that govern everything from the justice system to health care to regulatory bodies of every kind. Interestingly, recent surveys show that in Canada the degree of distrust in government institutions is more pronounced than in many other developed countries, including the United States. This is surprising considering the existence of strong regional identities in the United States and its history of bitter conflicts between state and federal governments over everything from civil and religious rights to abortion. Also striking, the same studies reveal that Canadians are far more likely than Americans or Europeans to rank local and regional governments as more trustworthy than their national counterparts. In comparison studies of seventeen advanced democratic societies in the past decade, Canadians rank thirteenth behind the U.S., Germany, France and the United Kingdom in terms of their confidence in key national institutions such as parliament.

Not surprisingly, declining levels of confidence in their federal institutions correspond to Canadians' changing terms of self-identification. Between 1990 and 2007, roughly the same number of Canadians, approximately 40 percent, said they identified first and foremost with Canada, the country. However, Canadians' sense of belonging or attachment to their province or region was up from 16 percent to 26 percent over the same time period. Translated into raw numbers, this means that some six million Canadian adults identify most closely with their province or region. This trend is evident not only in Quebec but in Alberta, British Columbia and Ontario as well. In all three English-speaking provinces, in 2007, compared with 1990, residents were up to a third more likely to identify first and foremost with their province than with the nation of Canada.

If Canadians exhibit lower levels of formal political participation, lose trust in federal institutions and more frequently identify with their province or region, then where are they finding community in their day-to-day lives? If it is not through reinforcing the common bonds of nationhood or the fulfillment of formal civic obligations, then how are Canadians satisfying the universal need to belong to something larger than themselves?

Proponents of the unencumbered-country concept would argue that Canadians have sensibly shifted their loyalties away from remote government institutions and an ineffectual democratic process to issues and methods that resonate with their individual values and interests. Peter C. Newman described the shift this way: "Instead of remaining yoked to the civic virtues of deference and self-denial which have held us back for so many generations, Canadians will follow an ethic of personal fulfillment that stresses self-reliance, autonomy, questioning of established authority…" In terms of new and emerging forms of social behaviour, this transformation has supposedly empowered community and advocacy organizations and created an upsurge in volunteerism, charitable giving, local involvement and non-traditional political engagement—everything from Internet activism to public demonstrations, petition writing and consumer boycotts—among Canadians generally and younger age groups in particular.

On the surface, the numbers associated with Canadians' growing investment in social networks, as opposed to formal political engagement, are impressive. According to comprehensive studies undertaken earlier this decade, some 61 percent of our fellow citizens belong to at least one social group or organization. Somewhere in the order of one in four or one in three Canadians, depending on the study, offer their time to organizations as volunteers, and young people today reportedly volunteer with greater frequency than either their parents or grandparents—yet another sign of the generational shift away from formal kinds of civic engagement, such as voting, to the informal realm of membership in interest groups and local associations. As a substitute for or complement to direct participation in such networks and organizations, 85 percent of adult Canadians indicate they donate some money to a charity every year, creating total contributions of close to $9 billion annually.

One might conclude from these numbers that Canadians have made up for their lack of interest in formal politics and the traditional democratic processes by joining community groups or volunteering or engaging in new forms of political expression. In effect, the emotional locus of community—the desire to be part of a larger whole that reflects and enhances our individual identities—has shifted away from the nation proper and towards regional and local concerns, or our personal interests and passions. If this is the case, then it does raise the question of why individual citizens, and the country as a whole, should continue to invest in the institutions, symbols and traditions of a shared nationality. Why undertake the hard effort of building a consensual and common national identity when it is clear that the trend is toward forms of social attachment that are local and highly personal? For proponents of the concept of Canada as a postnational country, this is exactly the dynamic at work today.

The other major corollary of the postnational society, according to its advocates, is the rise of an ethic of tolerance towards cultural diversity. While it might seem glib to say that diversity is what unites Canadians, this is a widely held sentiment. In a 2005 Dominion Institute survey, one in four Canadians said that diversity was what "makes Canada unique as a country." Personal freedom was a distant second choice, with only one in ten Canadians choosing it as the value that makes Canada unique. Two other defining features—our geography and our health care system— were given top rank by only one in twenty and one in fifty respondents respectively.

Our embrace of diversity as the hallmark of Canadian society is surely as significant an attitudinal change as our dwindling interest in formal politics and our declining attachment to national institutions. Indeed, a number of commentators have been quick to link our increasing acceptance of social and cultural diversity to the decline of a traditional vision of nationhood. They believe that in increasingly pluralistic societies, strong national identities can, in fact, impede a country from becoming more cohesive. Institutions and customs that press citizens to assume substantive civic responsibilities—such as knowing something about their country's history, assuming civic obligations before participating in the political process or promoting, through the state and the schools, a set of common social values—risk running up against and underscoring differences between the country's regions and between newcomers and longer-settled groups.

In other words, by defining and then asserting the attributes of a common nationhood, Canadians supposedly run the risk of antagonizing pre-existing social and cultural differences to the point that they become sources of conflict. It is significant that this outlook is held not just by an academic fringe or the country's political and bureaucratic elites. As previously noted, a Dominion Institute survey found that fully one in three Canadians believe that "part of what makes Canada a successful society is the lack of a strong national identity that individuals and groups are expected to adopt."

Proponents of the unencumbered-country concept also argue that the decline of the traditional institutions and civic customs of Canadian nationhood during a period of increasing levels of social diversity has not weakened our social harmony. In a survey the Dominion Institute conducted in 2007, slightly more than half of all first-generation immigrants reported having a "strong sense of belonging" to the country—the same percentage as in the general Canadian population. Taken en masse, the likelihood that newcomers will self-identify as "Canadian" increases steadily with the amount of time they live in Canada. Newcomers also participate in Canadian society at roughly the same levels as longer-settled groups. They are almost as likely to vote in elections or volunteer in their communities; they follow politics, read newspapers and know as much about the democratic process as the Canadian-born. In other words, they pretty much conform to the Canadian average in these matters and are *not* the cause of the country's declining overall rates of political participation and civic-mindedness. Rather, like the majority of longer-settled Canadians, they, too, are skeptical of formal politics and more focussed on what matters in their day-to-day lives: their families, their local communities and their personal interests.

Layer the kinds of civically benign and socially enriching consequences of cultural diversity over our long-standing tradition of accommodating minority language and religious rights, and the argument that, in an era of globalization and societal change, the absence of a widely shared civic creed is becoming a positive asset, if not a precious gift, becomes very persuasive indeed. As John Ibbitson enthused, Canada "will be known throughout the world as the exemplar of what can be achieved when chauvinism gives way to accommodation, when obsessions with shared race, shared blood, [and] shared history are transcended by an infinity of permutations."

CIVIC SLACKERS

From a distance, the vision of Canada as a country unencumbered by a common history, by onerous civic responsibilities or by a strong sense of national identity has its appeal. Certainly it captures the effects of the social and cultural forces that are transforming Canada. But does it serve as a worthy aspiration for the country and what it should become? Rather than providing an innovative road map for how highly diverse and decentralized nations can succeed in the twenty-first century, the idea of Canada as an unencumbered country makes, I am convinced, a virtue of the fact that we are "tuning out" formal politics and shedding the responsibilities of the democratic process, that we are choosing less demanding and highly personalized concepts of community and belonging. Before casting off the traditional hallmarks of a strong national identity, we would do well to think about the long-term prognosis for a Canada that has depleted the reserves of civic literacy and social capital, built up over decades, even centuries, by our forebears.

Social capital is the lattice of informal networks and shared norms that allow individuals from different backgrounds to formulate and advance common objectives, be they economic, cultural or political. Robert Putnam, the political scientist who has pioneered the study of social capital, writes: "Life is easier in a community blessed with a substantial stock of social capital... When economic and political negotiation is embedded in dense networks of social interaction, incentives for opportunism are reduced. At the same time, networks of civic engagement embody past success at collaboration, which can serve as a cultural template for future collaboration."

Over the last two decades, researchers have come to believe that social capital plays an important, if not vital, role in liberal democratic societies. Whether the problem is finding a job, creating a neighbourhood watch committee or lobbying a municipal government to reduce property taxes, social capital helps build trust between individuals and not only reinforces their shared values but provides the impetus for complex societies to pursue their common goals. While social capital can take many forms, it generally emerges out of communal activities, such as joining community groups or professional associations, becoming a member of a political party or movement, or volunteering to work in a church, with an international NGO or at the local food bank. Societies with low levels of social capital, even advanced democracies such as Canada, are thought to be prone to higher levels of political strife and to increased conflict between individuals and groups. Such societies find it difficult to resolve disputes informally and arrive at a consensus as to how to deal with internal crises and external threats.

In the case of Canada today, those seemingly rosy statistics regarding charitable giving, volunteering and non-traditional political participation are obscuring a raft of serious issues that could affect the long-term health of our civic culture. Specifically, markedly uneven levels of meaningful community involvement among all Canadians and the concentration of civic participation among an ever dwindling number of older citizens suggest that the country's reserves of social capital are anything but unlimited, and may, in fact, be in rapid decline.

Consider formal, ongoing volunteering and civic participation in Canada, two key measures of social capital. Between 1987 and 2006, the percentage of Canadians who were committed, long-term volunteers remained unchanged. But according to detailed analyses of volunteerism in Canada, a mere 10 percent of Canadians are responsible for upwards of 80 percent of all volunteer hours. The same disproportion obtains for donations to charities: one in five Canadians are responsible for approximately 80 percent of all money donated to charities.

A similarly discouraging ratio applies to civic participation measured by such activities as taking part in a demonstration, writing to a Member of Parliament or attending a community meeting. Somewhere in the order of 20 percent of Canadians are responsible for 65 percent of all civic participatory activities reported by our fellow citizens.

These different groups of socially engaged Canadians overlap in what is known as Canada's "civic core": the slightly more than 6 percent of Canadian adults who each year account for 42 percent of all volunteer hours, one in every three dollars donated to charity, and 20 percent of all civic participation.

Join the dots of these statistics, and the picture that emerges runs completely counter to our own self-image as "caring Canadians." The majority of us are civic slackers who participate either marginally, or not at all, in the kinds of formal activities that sustain a vibrant and effective volunteer sector, a participatory political culture and an enriched community life. Put another way, a significant portion of the population is doing little in terms of day-to-day behaviour to renew the social capital upon which much of the prosperity and social harmony of Canada depends today and into the future.

The same research shows that Canada's civic core is, at this point in our history, disproportionately comprised of older citizens, a finding that suggests formal volunteering and civic participation could be vulnerable to the same generational shift that has led to lower voting rates and decreased trust in public institutions. Such a shift could have a significant impact on our local communities. It is worth remembering that as recently as the 1970s, approximately one in five Canadians belonged to a service organization, such as the Legion, the Rotary Club or the Lions. These community-based groups play a vital role in towns and cities, helping organize local fundraising drives and volunteer activities for a range of important causes. By physically bringing people together around shared goals and values, service clubs create the kinds of deep and lasting social networks that make one's local community an enjoyable and enriching place to live. Today, as compared with thirty years ago, the number of Canadians reporting membership in a service group has almost halved to just slightly more than one in ten.

At the same time, participation in advocacy organizations where there are few, if any, substantive obligations attached to membership, other than perhaps reading a semi-annual newsletter or writing a cheque, has skyrocketed. In this context, Toronto's recent claim to being the city with the most Facebook members worldwide may be a by-product of its low overall levels of social capital. If you live in an environment where none, if any, of your peers belongs to a local community association or service club, then Facebook or any of a host of gaming sites, personal blogs or Second Life virtual realities can quickly become not just add-ons to your daily life, but the predominant means of maintaining a social network, however deracinated and transitory it may be.

It is not surprising that in terms of overall social interaction, Canadians today are spending more time alone than ever before. We enjoy 20 percent less time each day with our families than we did in 1985, and 50 percent less time with our friends. The amount of time we spend alone, outside of work, has increased by 25 percent in the last two decades and now averages some three hours each day.

It is also important to note that while Canada might be one of the most ethnically diverse countries in the Western world, the social networks that we take part in on a day-to-day basis consist primarily of people who claim the same ethnicity or ancestry. At the Dominion Institute we were surprised to find in 2007 that 58 percent of Canadians reported that all or most of their friends were of the same racial or cultural background, an indication that the majority of our personal relationships are with people who "look like us." The same survey also revealed that the social networks of second-generation Canadians were only half as diverse as those of newcomers to Canada. This finding suggests that the process of "integrating" into Canadian society entails a narrowing of social networks by race and ethnicity, not the broadening of cultural horizons that multiculturalism promised.

The uncomfortable truth for Canada today is that highly diverse societies traditionally experience lower levels of interpersonal trust and less faith in the efficacy of civic groups and institutions. As Robert Putnam discovered to his chagrin, communities that are ethnically and racially diverse are more likely to "expect the worst from their…leaders, to volunteer less, give less to charity and work on community projects less often, to register to vote less, to agitate for social reform more but have less faith that they can actually make a difference…." In other words, while increasing cultural diversity is a positive thing in terms of making local communities more interesting and socially rich, it is not an unalloyed good. The explosion of diversity in Canada's major urban centres adds another dimension to the challenge of shoring up the nation's reserves of social capital.

Finally, an examination of how civically engaged Canadians are should include some international comparisons. With respect to a range of indicators related to civic engagement and social capital, Canada is a statistical outlier among its peer nations. Australians and Americans are twice as likely to be active members of voluntary groups and service organizations. Many European nations, in particular the Scandinavian countries that have liberal welfare cultures similar to Canada's, enjoy higher rates of participation in non-formal political activism, such as attending demonstrations or public meetings, regularly discussing politics, signing a petition or writing to an elected official.

These facts paint a very different picture of the destination we could arrive at when the idea of a shared vision of Canadian nationhood is left behind in the dust of the postnational stampede. Instead of finding ourselves comfortable in local communities where our need to belong is satisfied by interaction with individuals and groups who share our interests and concerns, we may end up living mostly private lives cut off from the wider sources of community attachment and ever more confined to our immediate ethnic, regional or socio-economic enclaves.

A NATION OF AMNESIACS

In addition to being concerned about the decline in the kinds of social behaviour and overall civic-mindedness that generate social capital, proponents of a postnational Canada might want to consider the long-term impact of Canadians' low levels of civic literacy. Specifically, as the country becomes more diverse and increasingly regionalized, the lack of a common body of civic knowledge about Canada and its component parts could undermine the social consensus that has allowed Canadians their pride in the country's diversity. To state the obvious, diversity and its necessary corollary, acceptance, are the products of understanding. If as citizens we do not possess certain minimal levels of knowledge about each other and the larger civic institutions within which we interact, it will be difficult to sustain the national self-awareness and those shared values that support our way of life.

On this score, Canadians have, in comparison with other advanced democratic societies, some serious catching up to do. For instance, in 2001 the Dominion Institute surveyed Americans and Canadians on their knowledge of basic civic and historical facts about their respective countries. The kinds of questions we asked were such proverbial no-brainers as, who was Canada's first prime minister or who was the United States' first president? What is the name of that part of the Constitution that guarantees citizens their basic rights and freedoms? Our goal was not to trip up respondents, but rather to gauge how much they knew about ten simple political concepts and key historical facts.

We found that just slightly more than 60 percent of Americans passed their quiz, compared with a dismal 39 percent of Canadians able to pass theirs. Some will discount such a comparison on the grounds that American society has a long tradition of teaching its history and civics through its schools and popular culture. But it is worth remembering how diverse America is in terms of its strong regional cultures, its racial divide and its fast-growing Hispanic population. What allows such a society to function, despite its deep economic and class divisions, is the degree to which its citizens and national institutions take on the responsibility of maintaining a common set of civic touchstones that help define who they are as a people.

Furthermore, younger age groups in Canada have lower levels of awareness of political geography compared with those of other advanced democracies. When presented in 2002 with fifty-odd questions, including a test to identify countries on a world map, a sampling of Canadians aged 18 to 24 could answer less than half correctly. Overall, we placed seventh out of nine participating countries, well behind Germany and Italy and only slightly ahead of Mexico, a country not known for the high quality of its public schools.

One last finding: it is pretty well conclusive that what civic knowledge we do share is declining with time. As mentioned earlier, when the Dominion Institute was launched in 1997, we commissioned a survey modelled on the federal government's citizenship exam. Slightly less than half of those sampled failed our simple twenty-question quiz. Ten years later, on July 1, 2007, we released the results of an identical survey. This time, two in three respondents flunked the quiz, with the greatest decline in knowledge over the decade being registered in the eighteen-to-twenty-four-year-old age group. Not only do Canadians have relatively low levels of civic literacy, we seem to be fast shedding, with little concern, the remaining knowledge we do possess about the country's proud democratic history, its basic political customs and many of its key institutions.

While studies such as these provide at best a snapshot of Canadians' comparative civic knowledge, their findings dovetail with a larger body of research that indicates that there is a connection between our dwindling engagement with formal politics and our declining civic literacy. To me this makes sense. If we are shifting the focus of our attention and commitment away from Canada as a whole towards personal issues and local concerns, the impetus

to sustain a broad base of knowledge about the country's democratic institutions and civic traditions in our schools and popular
culture is bound to wither.

However, just as a falling stock of social capital can adversely
affect the ability of groups and individuals to pursue common
aims, a shrinking reserve of civic literacy will impede communi-
cation between us as citizens and as members of different social,
regional and cultural groups. It is not simply that by casting off
the building blocks of civic literacy we are in danger of becoming
a nation of amnesiacs; arguably, this process is already well
underway. Rather, in the not-so-distant future we could wake up
to find that we are strangers in a strange land, a loose assembly of
disparate peoples with few common experiences of any lasting
resonance or deep significance and little in common but the latest Canadian Idol contest or Weather Network report.

. . .

I would argue that without a shared national vision and without
common, widely held civic values, the self-congratulatory image
of Canadians as a socially diverse people who enjoy enviable personal liberty and freedom will not last. It is not clear to me that
our journey away from formal politics and traditional institutions
and symbols of nationhood will end in a society in which high
levels of social tolerance and mutual understanding continue to
support increasing diversity and political decentralization. Instead,
we could be on a collective voyage to a much darker destination.

One can easily imagine a Canada where we continue to neglect
our social capital and civic literacy and as a result lose not only
the capacity to forge common goals between diverse groups but
also the common reference points required to communicate and
articulate those goals. By failing to appreciate the extent to which
the tolerance of social differences is the product of underlying

cultural norms and networks of trust, a future Canada could see its once rich regional and linguistic tapestry unravel as individuals retreat into communities dedicated first and foremost to the interests of their immediate families or their ethnic and cultural groups. In effect, the vision of Canada as an unencumbered country where tolerance and diversity thrive in the absence of a single "Canadian" identity could soon find itself replaced by a collection of unencumbered individuals, an amalgam of intolerant and isolated people, all steadfastly committed to their own interests and their own self-affirming prejudices.

3 | FUTURE SHOCKS

THOSE who promote the idea of Canada as the world's first unencumbered nation will very likely shrug off my fears about loss of community or sense of connection to a public life of larger meaning. They will point to Canada's social harmony in a world echoing with the clash of civilizations, and to the overall personal well-being that Canadians report, sentiments that emerge in the same surveys that reveal our declining levels of civic engagement and shared knowledge. They will assert that in matters of domestic cohesion, we are entering an age where the traditional norms of national identity and individual belonging not only don't apply but have become impediments to the country's development.

Even if all this were true and if the concern I and others have about the country's declining reserves of social capital and civic literacy is nostalgia for a bygone era, there is another fact that cannot be dismissed. Canada is fast losing its relative isolation from the forces transforming our world—and as new threats emerge, our postnational country and its anemic national institutions will have to rise to the challenge, ready or not.

For much of the second half of the twentieth century, Canadians were largely protected from the direct impact of foreign conflicts. Yes, we were affected by the Cold War and took active roles in the Korean War, the Suez Crisis and numerous peace-keeping operations, but compared with our southern neighbour, our European allies and certainly much of the developing world, we passed those decades sheltered from the full sweep of world events.

This was partly due to geography. Living in North America's fireproof attic, above the world's largest crisis response team—the U.S. military—Canadians were able to pick and choose among the crises we would try to address or resolve. Among the more prominent in our recent past were the international campaign against apartheid, the UN treaty to ban landmines, the first Gulf War and the NATO intervention to help end the civil war in the former Yugoslavia. While we are loathe to admit it, Canada's distance from the major conflagrations of the postwar era has also been a function of conscious choice. Paltry foreign aid budgets, an increasingly ineffectual diplomatic corps and, until recently, a woefully underfunded military flowed largely from the fact that Canada faced no serious external threats to its existence. Instead, the country enjoyed a surfeit of options as to how, when and where we would engage with the wider world and its problems.

The churn of global events caught up with Canada on September 11, 2001, when twenty-four of our fellow citizens died in the spectacular terrorist attacks on the World Trade Center in New York. Setting into motion the invasion and occupation of Afghanistan and Iraq and signalling the rise of Islamic extremism as a terrorist threat, 9/11 foisted on Canada a series of intractable issues whose resolution is vital to the future peace and prosperity of the country. How, for instance, can Canada and the international community rebuild Afghanistan's civil and political institutions while at the same time fighting a counter-insurgency war against the Taliban? Will it be possible to maintain the free flow of goods and people across the Canada-U.S. border in the face of America's demands for greater homeland security? What is the future of multiculturalism in a world where religious hatred all too often trumps belief in liberal democracy and pluralism, sometimes with deadly results?

This last question points to a particular quandary: whether it is the systemic poverty that grips much of the developing world, or the way the Internet has been used to radicalize young Muslims in non-Arab countries, liberal democracies included, or the tendency of corrupt Arab regimes to buy off internal dissent by fomenting *jihad* beyond their borders, most of the factors that make radical Islam the threat it is today lie beyond Canada's ability to influence, let alone stop. In the face of our relative powerlessness to alleviate the root causes of terrorism, Canadians must, for the foreseeable future, sustain small but deadly wars that have no clear end, such as the one in Afghanistan, as well as endure the multiple predicaments of managing relations with a neighbour justifiably obsessed with preventing another terrorist attack on its soil.

The events of September 11, 2001, and the fallout from the "War on Terror," however, are only the tip of the proverbial iceberg of forces that could fundamentally transform our society. There are two unavoidable challenges we will confront in the decades ahead. First, climate change has the potential to wreak havoc on the global commons, including Canada's natural environment and its economy. Second, our rapidly aging population presents us with a bundle of interconnected problems that will overturn many of our assumptions about how and why Canada works. These issues have the potential to span generations. They originate in events and trends that lie outside of our ability to manage or control.

So before we discount the importance of shared historical memory, widely accepted values and a commitment to national identity as anachronisms of an outmoded "nation-state," it is worth considering what the future may hold for Canada. We need to think carefully about whether or not the type, scale and complexity of the issues that will define that future can be managed by a society in which identities, values and institutions are flexible and fluid. After decades of relative complacency, are we at risk of jettisoning the cultural capital which could prove decisive in making common cause and meeting these issues head-on? Will our diminished levels of social solidarity be able to sustain the country if it is gripped by a prolonged crisis? Global warming and an aging population are just two issues that will inevitably test our ability to formulate long-term national goals and make collective sacrifices for future generations.

DEMOGRAPHICS IS DESTINY

Canadians love Florida. The long, sandy beaches, the sprawling interstate highways, the vast shopping centres and the bustling streets of multi-ethnic Miami are just a few of the Sunshine State's prime attractions. But obviously, most important to winter-weary Canadians is the reliably warm weather, in itself a draw that has made Florida one of our favourite foreign destinations.

Irrespective of how many Canadians visit or live temporarily in Florida every year, familiarity with America's most southern state is useful in discerning what lies ahead for Canada. No, I don't think Canada's near-term future includes hurricanes and rising sea levels, rampant illegal immigration or a full-on, Florida-style meltdown in housing prices. Rather, Florida can serve as a snapshot of a fast-aging society; that is what makes it instructive—and alarming.

We all know, or can easily imagine, what it is like pulling off Florida's Interstate 95 into a Denny's restaurant to catch the early-bird special. The first thing one notices is not the oversized food portions or the occasional Confederate flag on a baseball cap; it is the advanced age of one's fellow diners. One in five Floridians today is over the age of sixty-five, and this graying of the state has already had a major impact on the quality of life of Florida's poor and needy as well as on the future spending capacity of federal and state governments. Florida has the third-highest per capita Medicare costs (Medicare being the U.S. health insurance program primarily for people over sixty-five years of age) in all of America. Prescription drug sales in Florida are also among the highest in the United States on a per capita basis, totaling some $10 billion annually. The endless health-themed malls, each chock-a-block with private clinics for cataract surgery or cancer treatments alongside supersized pharmacies, are the hallmarks of a society where advanced age is not just a demographic reality—but a very big business.

But the real challenge posed to policy-makers by Florida's graying population is not spiralling health care budgets. It is the lost revenue that results from a shrinking workforce. Most, perhaps all, of the elderly patrons at the Denny's I've frequented were enjoying not only the meatloaf and coffee but permanent retirement, too. Florida has the fewest people of working age of any state in the U.S. In other words, it has the least number of full-time workers whose taxes can be used to pay for the social entitlements and benefits of those aged sixty-five and over, or eighteen and under. Even with access to federal Medicare funding and direct transfers for various social programs, public education and city infrastructure, even with cheap and primarily illegal immigrant labour, Florida's diminishing workforce and declining tax revenues have forced its legislators to claw back health care benefits and long-established social programs.

What does the graying of Florida today have to do with Canada tomorrow? Isn't Canada, as our politicians always tell us, a "young country"? Isn't one of the many benefits of our policy of sustained, high immigration levels a youthful population that can pay the taxes that will be required to take care of the country's fast-retiring baby boomers? In 2020—eleven short years from now—the average age of Canadians will be that of Floridians today. In addition to the Tim Hortons outlets filled with retirees enjoying soup and sandwich combos and the malls catering to a full range of goods and services for the elderly, Canada, like Florida, will face ballooning government budgets driven by the costs of health care, social services and pensions for senior citizens. To quote Université du Québec economist Pierre Fortin, "The passage of baby boomers to old age is not weather forecasting. It is for certain. And the amount of the tab that they are going to leave us with is both large and unavoidable."

Economists conservatively estimate that as the percentage of the Canadian population over the age of sixty-five increases from 13 percent in 2009 to roughly 18 percent by 2020, the resulting demographic shift could easily end up costing taxpayers $50 billion annually. Let's examine that figure. First, seniors generate, on average, five times the health-care-and-social-services-related expenditures of younger adults. Given that Canada's federal and provincial governments combined currently spend approximately $100 billion a year on health care and social services, a very modest annual increase of 2.2 percent in spending in these two areas would cost, by 2020, $25 billion annually—an estimate well below current year-to-year increases in social services and health care spending. This number also does not factor in the ongoing advances in the medical life sciences, which are extending Canadians' longevity in the final, and from a health care perspective most expensive, years of their lives. In British Columbia, for example, the government spends approximately $2,000 per year on health care for every citizen aged fifty to fifty-five, compared with a whopping $22,074 annually for each B.C. senior ninety and older. In short, my $25 billion per year could well prove to be a low-end estimate of the new health care and social services spending that will be required by the year 2020.

As more Canadians become retirees and those already in their later years live longer, spending on the Canada Pension Plan and old-age security programs will also increase. Just eleven years from now, the additional 5 percent of the Canadian population over the age of sixty-five will receive $12 billion more annually in pension payments.

However, my tally of $37 billion annually by 2020 for the graying of Canada is still short of the economists' estimate by $10 billion or so. Where is the missing money?

Like Florida, Canada will soon confront the financial consequences of a shrinking workforce. On January 1, 2012, the first baby boomer born in Canada—part of one of the biggest postwar baby booms of any developed country—will retire. In subsequent years, the exodus of boomers from the workforce will accelerate. Unfortunately for many modern industrial nations, Canada included, population growth flattened after the last baby boomer was born in 1966, and then declined precipitously. Today, Canadian women are giving birth, on average, to 1.5 babies each—half a child short of population replacement. By 2020, the whipsaw of ever more retirees and ever fewer people entering the workforce will begin to bite. Taking into account the fact that some seniors are working past the age of sixty-five, conservative estimates project a four-percent drop in the overall employment level and an annual loss in tax revenues of $10 billion. Add the estimated increase of $37 billion in new spending on health care and social services for seniors to $10 billion in lost taxes, and you are close to $50 billion a year in new government spending. To put this amount in context, if governments had to plug an equivalent hole in their budgets today, they would have to levy $2,300 in new taxes annually on every adult Canadian.

If we cast our minds ahead to the year 2035, just as I am reaching the age of retirement and starting to look forward to spending some of my winters on a beach in Florida (climate change and sea levels permitting), it is all but inevitable that most, if not all, of the entitlements that make retirement possible today for the vast majority of sixty-five-year-old Canadians will have disappeared. More precisely, they will have been consumed by the growing disparity between the number of full-time, tax-paying employees and those too aged or infirm to work as the country tries to get by with having only two workers for every retiree, as compared with four workers today.

We should not underestimate the implications of a grayer Canada for the preservation of basic social equity and intergenerational harmony and of those social programs and conventions we have adopted to differentiate ourselves from the United States. Nor can we shrink from the difficult truth that the demographic train has left the station; no easy solution exists to halt or reverse this phenomenon. Increasing fertility rates would be the ideal long-term response, but countries such as France and Germany, which are also experiencing below-population-replacement birthrates, have largely failed to persuade women to have more children, despite offering generous child benefits. The fact is that low birth rates have become a corollary of modern life in most Western nations and much of Asia. The exceptions that stand out are New Zealand, Iceland and the United States, where two factors that are conspicuously absent in present-day Canada—high levels of religiosity and comparatively low levels of urbanization— seem to contribute to higher birth rates.

What about Florida's example of shifting the cost and responsibility for an aging society from the state to the individual? Or, before considering such drastic measures as privatized health care and radically curtailed pension benefits, what if we simply extended the age of retirement from sixty-five to seventy years or more? People are living longer than before and more of them are engaged in office or technical work, not manual labour. Indeed, studies do show that raising the retirement age will moderate the financial consequences of mass retirement by the baby-boom generation: the shrinkage in the workforce slows, which keeps the ratio of tax-paying workers to benefit-consuming retirees at manageable levels.

In my view, it is unlikely that our political leaders will adopt the idea of postponing the payout of old-age benefits any time soon, let alone cut back pensions or make health care costs an individual responsibility. Remember, four-fifths of Canadians over the age of sixty vote in elections, as opposed to less than one-third under the age of thirty. Telling this group of high-turnout voters that they have to punch the clock for another half decade or more for the good of the truly elderly and the very young is a guaranteed way for farsighted and courageous governments to lose elections. Furthermore, extending the retirement age just postpones the inevitable. Even if older Canadians were suddenly gripped with an overwhelming sense of intergenerational responsibility and agreed to defer the entitlements that come with retirement by five years, studies indicate that the size of Canada's workforce will start to decline in 2030 and then shrink rapidly as our ever more aged population shuffles over the half-century mark.

The one surefire way to increase the size of Canada's workforce is immigration. Thanks to increased numbers of new arrivals, the country's population growth—a blistering 5.4 percent over the last five years—is currently the highest among the G8 industrial-ized countries. By bringing in some quarter-million immigrants, or 0.8 percent of Canada's entire adult population, each year, we are more than making up for the population deficit created by our flaccid national birthrate. According to the 2006 census data, only 400,000 Canadians were born in Canada between 2001 and 2006, compared with 1.2 million immigrants settling in the country during the same period. So we seem to have found the silver bullet. As more Canadians reach the age of sixty-five and jet off to Florida or Arizona for the winter, we simply adjust immigration rates to ensure we continue to have four workers for every one retiree. To some extent, this is already happening. By 2010, newcomers will account for all of the country's net workforce growth.

But is immigration really the cure-all for Canada's demographic woes and the answer to driving down the average age of our population? Probably not. It turns out that newcomers are on average only slightly younger than the resident population. Research shows conclusively that there is no significant difference between the age structure of the quarter-million immigrants who came to Canada in 2008 and the population as a whole. Moreover, the trend is for the average age of newcomers to increase as the populations of those countries that send immigrants to Canada, such as China, Korea and the nations of Eastern Europe, also age. By virtue of their similar age and cultural attitudes about reproduction, women who immigrate to Canada have fertility rates that are not so different from the national average.

This is not to criticize immigration as a strategy for coping with an aging population. Welcoming large numbers of people to Canada is the most effective way of sustaining a national workforce and a tax base capable of supporting the various benefits that make the country a fair and humane place to live. But we do have to bear in mind the implications of the average age and the birth rates of recent newcomers and resident Canadians being similar. The fact is that if Canada wants to use immigration to maintain its current ratio of four workers for every one retiree from now through to 2030, then we should immediately increase our annual intake of newcomers from the current 260,000 individuals to approximately one million.

Economists calculate we would need to keep immigrations levels at or above 3.5 percent of the total Canadian population every year in order to continue to have four workers paying taxes for every one retiree by 2030. In other words, to keep the age structure of our population constant and our much-loved entitlements flowing, we as a country would have to increase our population from 33 million to some 57 million people—almost all through immigration—by 2020, a mere eleven years hence.

Mass immigration on this scale would transform the country. Remember that Montreal, Toronto and Vancouver together already absorb 70 percent of Canada's total annual immigration. Canada's urban population numbers would soar into the stratosphere or, more precisely, the country's suburbs would explode while growth in city cores stalled or reversed itself. This trend is already evident in cities such as Surrey and Kelowna, which have enjoyed growth rates twice that of Vancouver in recent years. In Ontario, the shift is even more pronounced, with the old city of Toronto registering a one-percent population growth between 2001 and 2006 while outlying suburban centres such as the once-rural town of Milton have experienced booming growth rates of over 70 percent.

In addition to the overwhelming social impact of mass immigration to the edge cities surrounding the country's largest urban centres, consider the very different economic circumstances newcomers to Canada will face, compared with earlier arrivals. Recent studies show that despite a decade of strong economic growth, fully one in three recent immigrants experiences a state of chronic low income, circumstances defined as a family of four living on $26,800 or less annually. Thanks to pervasive barriers to skills accreditation and an immigration system out of sync with labour markets, we are failing to create the kinds of economic opportunities afforded previous generations of newcomers. If we look ahead to a future where the country takes in a million or more souls a year and plunks them down in sprawling urban centres, it is not hard to imagine megacities such as Toronto and Vancouver transforming themselves, within a generation, into what journalist and author Daniel Stoffman has described as "São Paolos of the North." In vast suburb-ringed cities, growing numbers of economically dispossessed newcomers will have to fend as best they can while the country's public institutions, including its once prized health care and social services systems, are strained as never before.

Despite being provocative here with an extreme scenario of a million-plus immigrants a year, I want to emphasize the point that Canada's demographic die was cast in 1966 when the last boomer was born and birth rates started to decline. The most politically palatable and effective short-term solution to the country's shrinking workforce and tax base is dramatically higher immigration levels. They could well become a reality at the very time that the country is in the thrall of a postnational vision of a Canada that has declared a strong sense of national identity and widely shared civic values as passé.

The relentless graying of Canada will pit the young against the old and newcomers against the long-settled; it will place many of the country's cherished institutions and social conventions in jeopardy and endanger our long-term prosperity. Add mass immigration to the mix of intercultural and intergenerational tensions coursing through the body politic, and it quickly becomes apparent how vital it is that Canadians maintain high levels of social cohesion. Far from being anachronistic or impeding the country's development, assuming substantive civic obligations, adopting shared values and mastering a body of common cultural knowledge will be essential to achieving the consensus and solidarity required to survive the divisive debates and hard choices that lie ahead.

HOTHOUSE NATION

I am a Kyoto skeptic. No, I don't think sun spots or cosmic rays are the cause of global warming. Nor do I believe that technology will save humankind from the environmental consequences of two centuries of Western industrialization. The production of vast quantities of cheap, clean energy through hydrogen fusion remains the stuff of science fiction, and according to the most optimistic projections, wind, tidal and solar power can meet only a fraction of our total energy needs. I certainly do not buy into the cyclical theory of global warming and cooling and the notion that fluctuating global temperatures in recent years signal that the world is on the brink of another Ice Age. It is lunacy to think that mankind could have emitted more than 300 billion metric tons of CO_2 into the atmosphere since the start of the industrial revolution without fundamentally changing the environment. In my view, the theories of climate-change deniers are as credible as the average creationist's denunciation of evolution.

The problem I have with international covenants to reduce greenhouse gas emissions, such as the Kyoto Protocol and its successor agreements, is the illusion of control they create when it comes to managing the effects of climate change. By including country-by-country targets for emission reductions, first for 2012 and then beyond, Kyoto-like agreements foster the perception that Canada and the world's major carbon emitters can mitigate the worse effects of climate change and thereby treat global warming as a manageable rather than a life-threatening condition.

How dramatically could climate change affect Canada by the mid-century mark, the point at which a child born today would be settling into middle age? The answer: significantly, given the evidence of an acceleration in the warming of the planet since the 1990s, the period when far too many of us lived energy-super-sized lifestyles. Since the scientific measurement of global temperatures first began in 1859, twelve of the thirteen years from 1995 to 2007 were the warmest on record. Higher temperatures are causing not only glaciers to melt but seawater to expand: the annual rise in the world's sea levels doubled between 1993 and 2003, compared with the average for the previous forty years. The surface temperatures of permafrost in the Arctic—the top layer of which acts as a blanket preventing the release of thousands of years' worth of stored biomass and methane gas—have risen in the past decade as much as four times faster than in the previous century. As shown in report after report, the effects of climate change are evident in falling fish stocks (a trend that could have severe repercussions for Canada's coastal fisheries), the intensity and duration of hurricanes and cyclones (another reason Florida might not be such a great place to vacation in the coming decades), drought and desertification in Africa and Central Asia (get ready for the mass emigration of large numbers of environmental refugees from the developing world) and the melting of the Arctic ice cap. So even before we debate how high global temperatures might rise over the next few decades or what, if any, cuts to greenhouse gases may be achieved under a new set of international protocols, the evidence says that more and accelerating environmental change is an inevitable part of our near-term future.

Although many are still convinced that the world community can head off the worst effects of global warming, the current attitudes of China and India with regard to greenhouse gas emissions suggest that our faith in individual conservation and successor agreements to the Kyoto Protocol is misplaced. The inconvenient truth is that both China and India have repeatedly indicated that they will not participate in any greenhouse gas reduction scheme that threatens their economic development. For these emerging economic juggernauts, the argument is simple: why shouldn't developing economies follow a process of industrialization similar to that of the West and enjoy, over time, the same social and economic benefits? Leaders of the world's developing nations also correctly point out that the vast majority of the greenhouse gases in the atmosphere were put there by Western countries. They argue that future carbon emission reductions should be calculated on the basis of each nation's release of CO_2 over the previous century or more. On these grounds, China and India's total greenhouse gas emissions do not even come close to the historic contributions of the United States, Canada and the major European nations.

When one considers that China has only just entered what economists characterize as its period of "light industrialization" and that India is not far behind, the potential impact of both on an already dangerously overheated planet soon becomes apparent. The culprits here are not the tens of millions of suddenly middle-class Indians and Chinese who might rush out to buy automobiles and consumer goods with their new-found wealth; rather, the problem is the fact that the industrial boom in both countries is being driven by that staple of nineteenth-century Western economies: coal. In 2007, China surpassed the U.S. as the world's leading CO_2 emitter a full decade ahead of schedule, while India is currently in the number four position.

During the first phase of the Kyoto Protocol—the period from 1995 to 2012—India and China will have constructed some eight hundred new coal-fired power plants. Of those operating today, less than a quarter are equipped with CO_2 scrubbing technology. By 2012, their total combined emissions are estimated to reach a staggering 2.5 billion tons of CO_2 annually. This figure could well prove to be an understatement. For starters, both states have a history of turning a blind eye to the construction of black-market coal-fired electrical power plants by private companies and local municipalities. Also, if the price of oil continues to remain above historical averages because of a plateauing global supply, countries such as China and India that have no large proven oil or natural gas reserves of their own will face huge pressures to dig into the one energy source that is in plentiful supply within their borders: coal. China alone is estimated to have coal reserves capable of supplying 75 percent of the country's electrical power needs, at current levels, for the next forty to forty-five years.

Compare these kinds of sobering statistics with the best-case scenario hoped for under the Kyoto Protocol for the period between 1995 and 2012: if every country that is a signatory to Kyoto met its reduction targets, global CO_2 emissions would be reduced by 500 million tons annually. The efforts of developed countries such as Canada to reduce their share of CO_2 emissions by 2012 and beyond—including the purchase of billions of dollars of carbon emissions credits and legislating steep CO_2 cuts for domestic industries and individual consumers—will pale beside the 2.5 billion tons in annual emissions produced as a result of India's and China's consumption of coal.

A host of other factors, including rapid industrialization in populous countries such as Indonesia and Brazil and an entrenched view in the developing world that greenhouse gas reductions should be based on a country's per capita rate and not its total emissions, make it impossible to believe that we stand a chance of meeting the Kyoto goal of stabilizing CO_2 concentrations in the atmosphere at anywhere close to 1990s levels, let alone preventing a significant rise in global temperatures.

It has been suggested that as the developing world begins to industrialize in earnest, global CO_2 emissions for the period between 2006 and 2030 could easily equal the volume of the entire twentieth century: a mind-boggling 267 billion metric tons. These kinds of emission levels could conceivably push CO_2 concentrations in the atmosphere from 450 parts per million today to in excess of 650 parts per million by the mid-century mark. This is the danger zone in terms of generating the potentially catastrophic outcomes associated with an increase of three degrees or more in global temperatures over pre-industrial levels: the extinction of a third or more of the planet's known species, the displacement of hundreds of millions of people by rising sea levels and drought, increasingly devastating and frequent hurricanes and cyclones and extended water and food shortages affecting up to a billion people, primarily in the world's poorest countries.

What does the prudent developed country do in such circumstances? Certainly, it should try to reduce its own greenhouse gas emissions, which in Canada's case currently count for about 2 percent of total global emissions. But it must also prepare for the possibility of sweeping environmental, political and economic change.

For Canada, higher average temperatures in the decades ahead will bring a raft of new environmental challenges and threats. The first battlefronts will be our major cities and their sprawling suburbs. Well before the year 2050, Canadians living in metropolitan Vancouver, Calgary, Toronto and Montreal—each with 5 to 8 million people—will be suffering through severe summer heat waves, high levels of ozone and increasingly deadly smog. Higher average temperatures will also mean lower water levels for Canada's major river systems, including the St. Lawrence, as well as the Great Lakes. As was seen in the late 1990s, significantly lower water levels in central Canada have the potential to disrupt hydroelectric power generation and choke the shipping arteries that are critical to the smooth functioning of our economy.

In Western Canada, warmer temperatures would initially drive up crop yields, but at the same time they could adversely affect snow and rainfall patterns in the Rockies and thereby reduce the flow in river systems that play a vital role in crop irrigation. There is also the likelihood of widespread insect infestations of Canada's forests, which in turn would fuel larger and more devastating fires in the interior of British Columbia and parts of Alberta.

In the Atlantic region, rising sea levels would increase the risk of wide-scale floods and coastal erosion. More devastating would be the acidification of the sea, the absorption of vast amounts of carbon by the oceans, which could severely damage already depleted fish stocks.

It goes without saying that Canada's Far North will be fundamentally transformed by global warming. In addition to the costs associated with supporting human settlement in a fast-changing environment, higher temperatures could have a major impact on the cost of extracting resources from the region's interior. Longer summer seasons would make it increasingly difficult to ship goods and heavy equipment via their usual routes: over winter roads built on permafrost. Warmer summers would also see foreign vessels using Canada's Arctic waterways as shipping routes, thereby requiring the federal government to assume new costs and risks to assert Canada's sovereignty over its sprawling northern territories.

The picture that emerges from these scenarios is not reassuring: if Canada experiences an increase of three degrees in average temperatures over pre-industrialized levels by 2050, it will suffer prolonged stresses affecting every region and multiple systems, be they economic, environmental or social. Beyond the massive financial burden associated with managing the effects of a warmer Canada—a price tag of potentially tens of billions each year—it is worth considering the pressures that localized, and in many cases intractable, environmental threats could exert on our political ecology, most notably on our decentralized federal system of government.

One can imagine a new "green divide" opening up between the country's carbon-rich and predominantly rural provinces, notably Alberta, and the three megacities of Vancouver, Toronto and Montreal, each depending on the health of energy-intensive manufacturing sectors and a sprawling urban infrastructure. For the former, efforts by other provinces or a national government to significantly reduce Canada's greenhouse gas emissions or control the extraction and commercialization of natural resources will be perceived as threats to their economic development. The reality is whatever short-term fluctuations might occur in the price of a barrel of oil on a year-to-year basis, the plateauing of the world's supply of hydrocarbons, combined with the relentless industrialization of the energy-hungry developing nations means that filling your car up will cost more not less in the coming decade. This historic trend towards higher commodity prices will further stoke a go-it-alone ethos among Canada's energy-rich provinces as the wealth generated through the exploitation of their natural resources will equip them with the financial means to bypass national programs and initiatives and provide for their own health care, infrastructure, education and other government spending needs.

The same forces that are emboldening these provinces will continue to work against the long-term prosperity of Vancouver, Toronto and Montreal. In the coming years, high commodity prices, especially for energy, will drive up manufacturing costs for Canadian companies already hobbled by low productivity and a

Canadian "petro" dollar that trades equal to or higher than the U.S. greenback. Our goods and services will become more expensive in international markets at the very time when India and China are producing high-tech products with lower labour and energy costs. The inevitable job losses, the decreased tax revenues and the exodus of head offices from the rust-belts around Toronto and Montreal will cause urban centres already fed up with national inaction on climate change and higher energy costs, by historical standards, to lash out at the country's energy-rich regions.

Those urban centres will not, however, be without options. With some 70 percent of all immigrants continuing to settle in the country's three largest metropolitan areas, the cities will begin to exert real political muscle and push their agenda onto the national stage. While dozens of new federal ridings are created in mushrooming urban areas, the population decline in rural Canada will lead to proportionally fewer seats in the federal parliament for the resource-rich regions. It is more than conceivable that in the next few decades Parliament and the major policy instruments of national government could become captive to an overtly urban agenda deeply at odds with that of the energy-producing provinces. How could the country's cities resist using the power of the ballot box, for example, to insist on steep reductions in greenhouse gas emissions or to legislate that a share of natural resource revenues goes directly to their coffers?

I think it all but inevitable that Canada will soon have to confront the consequences of a "green imbalance" in our political landscape. Far more complex and thorny than the fiscal-imbalance debates which dominated federal-provincial relations in the last decade, Canada's green imbalance, could, in a short period of time, set the interests of Canada's major urban centres and those of its resource-rich regions on a collision course.

A FORK IN THE ROAD

In the face of these potential threats, is this the right moment in our history to be embracing the notion that we are the world's first truly unencumbered country, a nation where the obligations of citizenship are more symbolic than real? What are the consequences of choosing to shed the broad-based political engagement and the sense of social solidarity that are capable of challenging individual self-interest in an era of onrushing demographic and climate change? How will we respond as a people and a nation? Global warming, like the graying of Canadian society, will place acute pressures on our national institutions and strain the social and political fabric of our highly decentralized federation. We could well be driven to rethink some of our most fundamental and long-held assumptions about how and why the country functions.

I believe that the multiple and shifting threats posed by these two issues could force us to reduce the complexity of our federation. With several levels of government performing the same functions and with a patchwork of rules and regulations created by ten provinces, each having jurisdiction over the environment, health care, natural resources, immigration and emergency preparedness, Canadians may find that the current trend toward decentralized decision-making and public institutions paralyzes our ability to adapt to the point where our quality of life is threatened. With regard to Canada's attempts to curb its CO_2 emissions, this dynamic is arguably already at work. Instead of having a single national strategy that harmonizes provincial efforts to address climate change with Canada's international commitments, we have, at the regional level, a hodgepodge of conflicting policies based on goals and assumptions that are independent of those of the government of Canada and the international community as a whole.

The transition to a more centralized and efficiently run federation will not be easy. It is not simply that globalization and free trade with the U.S. have strengthened the country's regions both culturally and economically at the expense of the federal government. An equally stubborn obstacle is Canadians' deep-seated cynicism about the efficacy of national institutions.

It is conceivable that a Canada stressed out by global warming, demographic change or a not yet fully anticipated national emergency, such as a full-blown global energy or financial crisis, could come to a fork in the road. One way would lead to a stronger, more unified nation where governments and citizens rally to meet a common threat, putting aside jealously guarded prerogatives in favour of collective action. The other way would end in a Canada that fractures along new fault lines: struggling cities versus resource-rich provinces; an urban immigrant underclass versus a wealthy elite that can buy its way out of overburdened public institutions; and those with entitlements versus those who can never hope to claim them. While I know which of these two Canadas I would prefer, it remains a question as to whether we have the wherewithal to reform our fragmented federation and prepare for an uncertain future.

If we don't, I suspect that Canadians born today will look back at their parents and grandparents with a mixture of envy and contempt. For them, the end of the twentieth century and the first few years of the twenty-first will seem a golden age, a time when governments enjoyed balanced budgets, when the elderly and the poor received benefits and services from public institutions as opposed to the charity of extended families or businesses in the private sector, when cities were desirable places to live and not vast and decaying wastelands plagued by smog, heat waves and a poverty-stricken underclass, and when our involvement in the major global crises of the day was a matter of choice rather than survival.

What will be most striking to future historians of Canada *circa* 2009 is the ad hoc nature of the country's conduct at home and abroad. Such historians would recognize that, largely indifferent to the issues that would transform it, Canada mostly deferred the difficult and long-term decisions; that groups and regions who clamoured for special powers and treatment were more often mollified than resisted; and that the embrace of a postnational concept of nationhood was less a matter of principle than the reflection of our general complacency.

We should not be surprised if our children and grandchildren, having lived through the social and economic fallout associated with the graying of the country and the effects of climate change, come to resent the cavalier attitude we took towards the calamities that shaped much of their adult lives. Not only did we fail to take the steps that might have better prepared the country for these difficulties, we left diminished reservoirs of social cohesion and national vision that might have helped them make their way in an uncertain world. We denied them the benefits of inherited wisdom—the lessons of history, the examples of forebears, the models of national strength—that we ourselves were given.

Canadians trying to hold the country together in the middle of the twenty-first century may regard us not as prescient stewards but as absentee landlords who, having neglected the country's foundations, weakened the entire national edifice at the very moment when the forces that would fundamentally transform Canada were being unleashed.

4 | PASSAGE TO CANADA

NO matter how great the threat posed by rapid climate change or how serious the consequences of the aging of our population, for most Canadians such issues lie at the distant horizon of a still fuzzy future. What grips us is the here and now, the forces affecting our lives today in new and at times unsettling ways. It is our proclivity to focus on the short term that leads me to raise one more phenomenon that has already transformed our society and will continue to do so in the immediate and foreseeable future: immigration.

In ways that we are only just starting to appreciate, Canada's immigration policies and settlement systems are fundamentally changing the country and calling into question many of our long-standing assumptions about the nation's goals and purposes. Any substantive discussion of whether or not our country is best served by a national identity that is less onerous in its civic obligations and more accommodating to individual choice and group differences has to consider immigration's ongoing impact.

My own views about immigration have been influenced by the experience of creating and overseeing the Dominion Institute's Passages to Canada program, a national speakers' bureau of high-achieving immigrants who talk with young people and newcomers about what it was like to pull up stakes in their native countries and make Canada their permanent home. Passages to Canada gave me the opportunity to learn first-hand about the life experiences of new Canadians—both triumphant and trying—and about the ways in which our immigration policies are affecting the lives of newcomers and the country as a whole.

What struck me in these exchanges was a growing frustration among newcomers with the discrepancies between the potential and promise of their adopted land and the hard realities they faced in making a new life here. Many recent immigrants are understandably fed up with the inability of governments, businesses and professional associations to find ways to recognize the skills and work experience of foreign-born professionals in a timely fashion, if at all. And they are concerned not only about the widening economic disparities between recent immigrants and longer-settled groups but also about the prospects for the next generation, especially those immigrant children growing up in low-income families with limited options and resources. Most important of all, newcomers point to the fact that Canada is failing to appreciate how the world beyond its borders is changing and why increasing numbers of immigrant families are questioning their decision to make it their lifelong place of residence. Economic globalization is prompting more and more immigrants, especially skilled workers, to compare what Canada offers them with the opportunities available in other countries, including their native lands.

This reality was forcefully brought home to me a couple of years ago by a man who had settled in Calgary in the early 1990s. He had arrived from India with his wife, two children and a newly minted engineering degree. When it proved impossible to find employment as an engineer because his foreign credentials were not recognized and he lacked Canadian work experience, he fell into a series of low-wage jobs. Going back to university to earn a Canadian degree was not an option since he was his family's sole breadwinner. His wife had given up looking for work because the cost of daycare for their children was greater than the income she could earn in a service industry job. The friends and extended family to whom they would normally have turned for child care support were an ocean away.

After a few cold Calgary winters stuck in their small apartment, they decided that she and their children would return to India to live in Mumbai with her grandparents and he would visit as often as their modest savings would allow. During these long absences, the couple kept in close touch by phone and email and he visited India as often as he could afford. On one trip to Mumbai he struck up a business partnership with a relative in the clothing export business. Soon he was importing Indian-made goods to Canada and was able to earn some much-needed extra money to supplement his meager Canadian income. To the casual observer he was a model immigrant, a man who was toughing it out in less than ideal circumstances and using his entrepreneurial skills and the family network to make a successful go of it in Canada.

But then, starting in the early 2000s, he observed that his Indian friends and relatives were thriving in that country's fast-expanding economy. Housing prices were soaring and well-paying office and technical jobs were being created in his hometown. His wife had found full-time employment in an uncle's computer store, and their two children, while still Canadian citizens, were excelling at a private school the likes of which he could never afford in Canada. He was the eldest son of aging parents in India, so helping them was becoming increasingly important. And he recognized, too, that his attachment to India, its sports, music, movies and politics, had not waned despite his long absence, thanks to satellite television and regular trips home. By comparison, much of Canadian culture and politics had seemed remote and inaccessible, a conversation between the country's long-settled groups about unfamiliar issues and debates from times past.

And then it happened. Returning to Canada from yet another visit to India, he realized that bustling and familiar Mumbai had become, in his mind's eye, the land of opportunity and that his adopted homeland had become a dead end. After spending the first twenty years of his life dreaming of escaping India to start anew and then struggling for fifteen years in Canada to make his ambitions a reality, he decided to return to India for good. He and his wife and their children cherished their Canadian citizenship and looked forward to returning to visit friends in Calgary, but his future now lay in Mumbai with its buoyant economy, family ties and a community life that had never stopped feeling familiar and comfortable.

Hearing this personal testimony impressed on me, like no government study or policy paper, the fundamental need to re-examine our assumptions about the immigration system and the institution of citizenship itself. For starters, we can no longer take for granted that recent immigrants will settle for what Canada offers in terms of economic opportunity. Nor can we be complacent about the degree to which technology and less expensive travel allow all of us to maintain close connections with distant family and friends and to find community where we choose to, as opposed to where we physically reside. Gone are the days when immigrants, along with everyone else, mostly consumed the same media and were exposed to the same news reports or sports spectacles or popular culture. Nor should it be a surprise if Canada begins to find it more difficult to retain the highly skilled workers who chose this country in the past. We continue to outsource the manufacturing jobs—jobs that once provided newcomers with a leg up the economic ladder here—to the very countries in which we are trying to recruit immigrants. The upshot is that these workers and their professional and managerial counterparts have a greater range of options about how and where they will live than ever before.

Making our immigration system work for both the country and recent immigrants is of vital national importance. The challenge is more than building a deep and lasting attachment to Canada, more than figuring out how to equip an ever more socially diverse and decentralized country with the necessary reserves of social solidarity and cultural capital. And the prize is greater than simply having a way to manage the transforming social and cultural dynamics created by record-high levels of immigration. For me the story of one man's journey from India to a new life in Canada that, in the final analysis, paled beside the advantages of his homeland gets at the heart of the debate about what our nation could and should become.

IMMIGRATION SUPERPOWER

Canadians have long taken pride in their open and generally humane immigration policies. Broad public approval for high levels of immigration is an affirmation of the oft-repeated mantra that, excepting Aboriginal peoples, "we are a nation of immigrants," a diverse lot drawn from successive waves of migrants, starting with the first tentative European settlements that opened up the continent in the 1600s.

However, pride in immigration and the resulting pluralism of twenty-first-century Canada—a hallmark of our national identity—flows from something larger than simple support for cultural diversity. While it must be acknowledged that high immigration levels, as deliberate government policy, are as much a reflection of party politics as an articulation of lofty visions for

Canada's present and future, the public's support for immigration can claim nobler antecedents. I believe Canadians' endorsement of high immigration over the last quarter century is in large part the expression of a latent national ambition, the conviction that Canada is an exceptional country different from the European powers and our American neighbours. In much the same way that previous generations looked to the country's natural resource wealth, its historic connection to Great Britain and its military prowess overseas as markers of Canadian eminence, Canadians today have embraced immigration as one of the key distinguishing features of national identity.

In the words of John Ralston Saul, "Canada gets very few kicks at the can of world interest, understanding and influence. Is there anything about us which really does interest the rest of the world? Yes. One thing." People everywhere are fascinated by our experiment: 250,000 new citizens sworn in every year. John Ralston Saul's important point here is that while on the world stage culture and history may be synonymous with, say, France, or technology with Finland and Japan, or free markets and entrepreneurship with the United States and Singapore, Canadians have chosen to define themselves in no small part through high immigration. This is all the more remarkable for a nation whose recent history has been typified by the moderation of its public policy and cautiousness towards bold national programs that transform the country.

On average, Canada welcomes roughly a quarter of a million immigrants and refugees annually. In terms of absolute numbers, that is a fraction of America's intake of approximately a million legal immigrants per annum—many of whom are already living in the U.S. and have decided to acquire formal citizenship. But measured on a per capita basis, Canada is the world leader, welcoming in recent times an average of 7 migrants per 1,000 population each year. This tops 6.2 migrants per 1,000 population for Australia and is well above 4.4 immigrants per 1,000 population in the United States. European immigration leaders such as Denmark, Holland and the United Kingdom post figures similar to those of the U.S. However, in terms of a percentage of the total population, Canada takes somewhere in the order of a third more legal newcomers annually than the United States and the handful of high immigration countries in Europe. And this is not new: we have welcomed more legal migrants to our shores on a per capita basis than any other country for almost two decades now, some five million souls since the mid-1980s.

The effects of prolonged high immigration on Canadian society have been dramatic. Over the past twenty years, the percentage of Canadians who are first-generation immigrants jumped from 16 percent in 1986 to fully one in five by 2006, the highest proportion in seventy-five years. The shift from primarily European immigration to immigration from Asia, the Middle East and South America in recent decades has drastically changed the racial complexion of Canada. As recently as 1970, the year of my birth, only one in a hundred Canadians was a visible minority; today it is closer to one in six.

Those living in the major urban centres will acknowledge these figures as the "new normal." Yet in comparison to other Western countries, the diversity of present-day Canada is nothing short of extraordinary. We forget that visible minorities make up almost 17 percent of the total population, compared with 15 percent in the United States, which includes a large and long-settled Black population, 12 percent in the United Kingdom and 10 percent in European countries such as the Netherlands. Canada's status as an immigration superpower is more pronounced when one compares the portion of the population that is foreign born in cities such as Toronto (46 percent) and Vancouver (40 percent) with the likes of Los Angeles, New York, London or Melbourne, where the percentage of foreign-born residents ranges between 27 and 36 percent. Within a single generation, immigration from increasingly non-European nations has made Canada one of the most ethnically diverse and socially complex societies in the world today, a country that stands out from other Western democracies for having enthusiastically accepted the cultural differences and social mores of newcomers.

European countries struggling to integrate their economically disadvantaged and culturally alienated immigrant underclasses perceive Canada as a country that foresaw, decades before other Western nations, that the mixing of peoples, religions and races within nation-states would be one of the great opportunities and challenges of a globalized world. Our integration and multiculturalism policies are studied by other countries as models for how societies that are being transformed by high immigration can reconcile social differences and promote tolerance. In Europe, and worldwide, this perception has enhanced Canada's image among its peer nations. Instead of being perceived solely as a resource-based country with some technological expertise and manufacturing ability, Canada has achieved the status of an immigration powerhouse that is winning us attention and accolades abroad.

Consider the international surveys that in recent years have consistently placed Canada among the top three countries with the most respected national "brand" among thirty-five nations worldwide. Not surprisingly, Canada's natural beauty is most often ranked number one in the same studies. However, with regard to immigration and the "openness" of the society and its people, we consistently vie for the number two slot beside the United Kingdom, the U.S. or Australia. In Asian surveys, Canadians are judged to be almost twice as tolerant as Australians and three times more so than the British—two culturally similar peoples whose countries also accept comparatively high numbers of Asian immigrants. It is interesting that from a list of the eight most attractive qualities a nation can have, Asian respondents identified social tolerance and the openness of individuals as being the most important. These two values-oriented characteristics beat out such factors as the prevailing business climate, the prevalence of advanced technology and a dynamic economy as desirable national characteristics. We are definitely on to something. Our immigration policy has given us a reputation as a country where diversity is both a competitive advantage and an expression of Canadian exceptionalism.

Among high-immigration nations, we enjoy one of the highest rates of formal citizenship acquisition for immigrants. In recent years, upwards of 84 percent of permanent residents have become full citizens, as compared with 75 percent in Australia, 56 percent in the United Kingdom and 40 percent in the United States, the country most often regarded as the world's most desired immigration destination. According to Dominion Institute research, first-generation immigrants are more likely to express greater levels of attachment to Canada than the general population and are more likely to identify with Canada, the country, as opposed to their region or local community.

While it is difficult to find equivalent studies in other Western democracies that quantify immigrants' levels of attachment to their adopted country, the growing debate over the long-term effects of immigration in Europe and the United States suggests that in those places there is a hardening of attitudes and a widening cultural divide among longer-settled groups and newcomers. In Canada, this has not yet happened. The Dominion Institute found in 2007 that first-generation immigrants, despite barriers of language and culture, knew more about Canadian history, geography and government than longer-settled groups. Studies by Ipsos Reid show that a strong majority of Canadians support current immigration levels and see newcomers as having a net positive effect on the country. While these kinds of findings do not allow for a definitive judgment, they do suggest that when it comes to such social indicators as the rate at which immigrants acquire Canadian citizenship, their level of attachment or sense of belonging to the country and their knowledge of their adopted homeland, newcomers are becoming "Canadian" in reassuring numbers. At the same time, the general public feels Canada is successfully integrating large numbers of new citizens.

FADING DREAMS

Theoretically Canada should be well positioned to compete for desirable immigrants in the decades ahead and better prepared than most countries to meet the challenges of continuing high levels of immigration. But let's go back to those immigrants who shared stories of their actual experiences. From their vantage point, Canada's record for successfully settling newcomers seems more faded dream than fact.

The statistics on the growing economic disparities between newcomers and longer-settled Canadians speak for themselves. While Canada recently experienced one of the strongest and most sustained economic expansions in its history—the country's economy has grown by 56 percent between 1990 and 2006—the number of immigrants living in poverty has risen dramatically. The percentage of recent immigrants whose family incomes fall below Statistics Canada's low-income benchmark has risen from 24 percent in 1980 to 31 percent in 1990 to 34.1 percent in 2006. During this same period, the low-income rates among the Canadian-born population overall declined from 17 percent to 11.4 percent. The increase in poverty among newcomers has occurred among all immigrant groups, even the highly skilled and highly educated. Only immigrants having lived in Canada for more than two decades avoided an increase in their overall poverty rate. And experts attribute the better economic performance of this group to the different labour markets and immigration policies that existed in the 1980s as much as to their longer residency.

The widening gap in prosperity cannot be blamed on lower skills or employability among new arrivals. The percentage of new immigrants with university degrees has increased from 17 percent in 1992 to close to 50 percent in recent years. Yet despite almost two decades of selecting immigrants with higher skill levels and greater expert knowledge, native-born Canadians earn fully one-third more than newcomers of the same age and similar education levels. Furthermore, declining earning power among new Canadians is a trend that seems to be intensifying. Newcomers with similar levels of foreign and Canadian work experience who came to Canada between 1995 and 1999 are earning on average 25 percent less than immigrants who arrived in the 1960s.

The likelihood of immigrants enduring prolonged periods of underemployment or low income is higher now than at any time in the country's recent history. And again, recent immigrants have experienced a diminishing of their earning power during a period when the country's unemployment levels were at their lowest in thirty years. Faced with the quandry of how they and their families will get by as Canada experiences its first major economic downturn in almost two decades it is no wonder recent immigrants protest the discounting of their foreign training and skills and the barriers which prevent them from utilizing their knowledge and experience.

But this is only half of the problem. Immigrants living in poverty for extended periods of time are starting to realize that their diminished prospects are likely to be passed on to their children. This is a profoundly disturbing trend that has the potential to undermine the universal immigrant credo that the sacrifices of the first generation are justified and made bearable by the successes of the next. For each new wave of immigrants, the second generation is the one that is expected to reap greater economic rewards, enjoy greater social acceptance and be integrated into the power structures of their adopted countries.

Multi-generational research shows that children who grow up living in poverty for an extended period of time run a statistically significant risk of being poor as adults, regardless of their parents' education levels and employment experience or the kind of neighbourhood in which they are raised. Poverty is, in effect, a hereditary disease. The effects of substandard schooling, the absence of easily available early childhood health care and the lack of additional family income to pay for anything beyond rent and food all combine to handicap the prospects of children who grow up in low-income households. For instance, one long-term study of Canadian children from birth to early adulthood revealed that as many as one in three children from low-income families had "delayed vocabulary development" whereas less than one in ten kids from high-income families displayed the same problem.

The children who make up the third or more of all recent immigrant families living at or below the low-income mark have the added disadvantage of parents who may not speak French or English and who are coping with the pressures that come with making their way in a new country. It certainly does not help immigrant children in Toronto, the city that attracts the majority of newcomers to Canada, that the percentage of elementary schools with English-as-a-second-language instructors has declined from 41 to 29 percent in the last decade while the number of students requiring such instruction has doubled. The failure of successive governments to provide a level playing field where these children can compete with their native-born peers is a nationwide phenomenon—and one that has huge social implications for the future.

General indifference to rising immigrant poverty levels is partly to blame for our neglect, but more directly culpable are the federal settlement programs that transfer funding to the provinces and to settlement groups to ease the integration of immigrants and their children. Unequal and highly political federal funding has seen Quebec, which accepts less than a fifth of all immigrants who come to Canada each year, receive as much as $4,000 per newcomer in federal funds annually. In contrast, Ontario and British Columbia, which welcome year after year two-thirds of all immigrants to Canada, received as little as $900 per immigrant until the middle of this decade. Consequently, for the last twenty years, two of the country's major urban centres, Vancouver and Toronto, have lacked the financial resources necessary to integrate, economically and socially, large numbers of new arrivals and their children, especially within city-funded school systems. The covenant between Canada and its growing immigrant population to ensure that the dreams of the first generation are realized by the second is breaking down, with the result that newcomers' loyalties to Canada are being tested as never before.

CULTURE CLASH?

As immigrants see their dreams of a better life for themselves and their children dim during a period of relative prosperity for everyone else, they are naturally questioning the "inclusiveness" of Canadian society and their own long-term commitment to the country. The central issue here is one that Canadians have traditionally shied away from when discussing their immigrant and settlement policies, namely the impact that race has on immigrant communities and on Canadian society as a whole.

The sources of Canadian immigration have shifted since the 1960s from primarily European countries to Asia, the Middle East and South America. Since the 1990s, approximately half of all newcomers to Canada have originated in Asia and the Pacific region and another quarter has come from Africa and the Middle East. The United States and Europe have contributed less than a fifth of all new immigrants. In other words, new Canadians today are overwhelmingly visible minorities. For immigrants, this means that the lens through which they view Canadian society's risks and opportunities has changed significantly from the early 1970s when official multiculturalism was introduced and only one in one hundred Canadians belonged to a visible minority. The challenge now is not simply to provide newcomers with the economic fundamentals to succeed and to accommodate immigrants' cultural differences within Canadian society. It is to bridge what are at times deep-seated racial divides and to create social solidarity between different ethnic groups.

According to an exhaustive study of immigrants' attitudes undertaken earlier this decade, one in three visible-minority immigrants who arrived in Canada in the early 1990s or later indicated that they have experienced racial discrimination within the past five years. This compares with one in ten white immigrants who arrived in the same time period and less than one in five Canadians overall who told the Dominion Institute in a 2005 survey that they had been the victims of discrimination at some point in their lives. Second-generation visible-minority immigrants, though born in Canada, were more likely to report that they had experienced racial discrimination in the previous five years than their parents. This was true for all groups of visible minorities, ranging from 35 percent of second-generation Chinese Canadians to 43 percent of children of South Asian immigrants and as many as 60 percent of second-generation Canadians who claimed Black ancestry.

My point here is not that Canada is becoming a more discriminatory society. Previous waves of immigrants, whether Catholic, Jewish, Eastern European or Irish, experienced significant economic and cultural discrimination as well, primarily at the hands of the established Protestant majority. What is different today is the increase in the percentage of Canadians who belong to visible minorities from one in a hundred in 1970 to one in six in 2009 as well as the rise of racial identity as a new—and, if other countries' experiences are any indication—all too intractable divide between newcomers and longer-settled groups.

The breadth and depth of this racial divide was uncovered by a major survey of over 30,000 newcomers conducted in 2003. Its results indicated that second-generation visible minorities had lower levels of social trust, attachment to Canada and overall life satisfaction than their first-generation counterparts—the group that, by virtue of having arrived first, would have had to struggle harder to integrate into Canadian society. Specifically, in response to the key measurements of how strong their "sense of belonging to Canada" was and how "satisfied they were with their life in general," second-generation visible minorities ranked themselves lower than recent immigrants. Within Canada's historically large South Asian immigrant community, members of the second-generation were fully 20 percent less likely to express a "strong" sense of belonging to Canada than their first-generation counterparts who had arrived after 1991.

Understandably, given these results, overall levels of social trust—the essential ingredient in the formation of social capital that allows diverse societies to articulate common goals—were also lower for second-generation South Asians and most other visible minority groups. By contrast, the overall sense of belonging, life satisfaction and social trust were either up significantly or remained unchanged for second-generation white Canadians. The prevailing sense of alienation among the children of visible-minority immigrants was captured by the study's finding that three-quarters of second-generation Canadians of white ancestry identified themselves as "Canadian," as compared with slightly more than half of second-generation visible minorities. Diminished economic opportunities, perceptions of discrimination and under-representation in the country's major public and private institutions are creating new racial fault lines in our society, and if left unchecked could threaten the country's ability to continue to successfully integrate large numbers of newcomers.

But lest we forget, integration is a two-way street. Immigrants need to adopt the basic values and civic practices of the host country in order to perpetuate the social norms of the larger culture that made that country a worthy or desirable emigration destination in the first place. In exchange, newcomers, like longer-settled groups, have every right to expect their adopted home to provide opportunities for economic and social advancement for them, if possible, but certainly for their children. In the absence of a major push to reaffirm a shared vision of citizenship, one that promotes equality of opportunity regardless of race, religion or creed, I fear this simple social contract is in danger of breaking down.

Indeed, it could be argued that Canada's international image as a nation united by diversity is in jeopardy. The number of ethnic enclaves in Canada—defined as communities with a third or more of the population consisting of a single visible minority—has ballooned since the 1980s, from only six such groupings in Montreal, Toronto and Vancouver combined in 1980 to 254 in the 2000s. But ethnic self-segregation is not a phenomenon of visible-minority communities alone. Anecdotal evidence suggests that small towns and communities ringing the country's major urban centres are the beneficiaries of suburban "white flight"—the migration of middle-and-upper-middle-class white families out of the older edge cities where visible minority immigrants are settling in increasing numbers. We are at risk of becoming a society separated physically along ethnic lines, with Canadians of European ancestry increasingly leading the charge towards self-segregation in gated U.S.-style exurban communities and rural enclaves.

This social fragmentation became clear to me when the Dominion Institute commissioned a survey in 2007 comparing the social networks of immigrants to those of the general Canadian population. We found that roughly one in three first-generation immigrants reported that "all" or "most of" their friends came from the same racial or cultural backgrounds as they themselves. Given that immigrants everywhere tend to congregate first with longer-settled members of the same background, it is not surprising that recent arrivals to Canada would seek out their immediate ethnic or cultural group. But especially noteworthy were the responses from second-generation Canadians and from the general population. Some 42 percent of the children of immigrants and 58 percent of all Canadians responded that all or most of their friends were of the same ethnic background. In other words, from one generation to the next immigrants are integrating, but the communities they are joining have a strong impulse towards self-segregation. These findings suggest that the pluralist dream of Canada as a nation of mixed-race neighbourhoods, a truly colour-blind society, is not something we can take for granted.

Pick your social indicator, whether it be the likelihood of having a neighbour who is from a different ethnic background or the number of members of visible minorities heading major Canadian-headquartered companies, sitting in Parliament, serving in the armed forces or being employed by the federal, provincial and municipal public services. None comes close to reflecting Canada's exploding racial diversity: by 2020, visible minorities are expected to comprise 20 percent of the population.

The growing racial divides in Canadian society—economic, social and political—have been exacerbated by a business-as-usual immigration policy that is having a negative impact on the country's long-term economic prospects. Confronted with what must seem like insurmountable barriers to the utilization of their skills and work experience and finding that Canada is not as welcoming a society as it might like to think it is, significant numbers of immigrants are voting with their feet and are simply leaving the country. Studies conducted over the course of consecutive decades show that four in ten male immigrants who come to Canada as skilled or professional workers now leave the country permanently within ten years—the very immigrants Canada needs to shore up its shrinking workforce. Anecdotal evidence suggests that many of those who remain because they do not have skills or knowledge they can sell on the international market are turning to their immediate ethnic groups to find economic opportunities and social acceptance, groups that are not only culturally familiar, but often defined by their shared religious beliefs.

Some of these creeds, not unlike those of the religious sects that arrived with earlier waves of immigration, are embraced by small but vocal minorities who are anything but sympathetic to liberal democratic values that stress social tolerance and individual rights, including gender equality and sexual preference. The recent public debates over the scope and validity of minority religious and cultural rights have created heightened tensions within ethnic communities themselves and have fed a perception among the larger Canadian population that high levels of immigration have become a threat to the broad social values that underpin Canadian society. Whether it is a question of young

Muslim women playing soccer in head scarves or young Sikh men wearing kirpans in school, the fear among longer-settled groups, especially in rural Canada and Quebec, is that the country has changed too much too fast.

It is not hard to imagine a dystopian future in which our once-vaunted multicultural society splinters into a patchwork of ethnic enclaves, each populated by a permanent immigrant underclass trapped in dead-end jobs and lacking the skills or opportunity to advance up the economic ladder here or leave the country for opportunities elsewhere. Facing systemic discrimination and cut off from the larger debates about the country's direction, an ever more alienated immigrant population will be inclined, as it is in Europe, to find solace and understanding in religious and cultural beliefs that stand in sharp contrast to the liberal values of mainstream society. There is a real risk that unless there is a concerted national effort to bridge the distances between newcomers and longer-settled Canadians, we could see the kind of political backlash against immigration that in Europe has launched a vicious circle of mutual recrimination and social strife.

THE NEW PEACEKEEPING

When it comes to integrating newcomers into society and accommodating social differences, Canada is—for the moment—miles ahead of Europe. There is that phenomenal 84-percent citizenship acquisition rate among newcomers. Also, unlike Europeans and Americans, three in four Canadians support continuing high rates of immigration, a proportion that has remained constant for two decades.

I believe the root problem with the country's immigration and settlement systems is not the kind or the number of immigrants Canada accepts. Rather it is our careless attitude towards our shared citizenship and our disregard for how our high immigration policy functions as a source of national pride and exceptionalism in the twenty-first century. Like so many other urgent issues that we seem incapable of addressing—our failure to get serious about kick-starting the greening of our economy, confronting the approaching crisis of an aging population and replenishing our falling reserves of social capital and civic literacy—we are dodging our collective responsibility to make mass immigration work. Out of approximately $200 billion in total federal program expenditures in 2008, one-third of one percent was allocated to help settle newcomers who arrived in Canada last year—an average of $3,300 per person. By way of comparison, $7,000 per person were spent on programs and services for the just over one million Canadians who claim Aboriginal descent in Canada, many of whom require the same kinds of educational and skills development assistance that immigrants do. In terms of per capita federal expenditures to help new immigrants integrate into the workforce, we lag behind other high-immigration countries such as Australia, Denmark and the United Kingdom. The fact is that successive governments have increased overall immigration rates while voters have tacitly agreed to allow them to run the country's settlement programs on the cheap.

Our immigration success story may soon go the way of our record in peacekeeping. Despite a Canadian contribution of less than two hundred troops, mostly military police, to United Nations peacekeeping operations in Haiti, the Balkans and East Timor in recent years, many Canadians still believe that we are a "nation of peacemakers" and that we continue to be recognized as such internationally. This myth endures despite fundamental changes to our military and to the very nature of armed conflicts in a post-9/11 world. Similarly, the astounding fact that 40 percent of skilled and professional male immigrants leave Canada for good within ten years of arriving in the country fails to register with Canadians because it contradicts our faith in the country's capacity to assimilate newcomers. But we cannot afford blind spots on this issue. For now, we are the world's leader in per capita legal immigration, yet we must not underestimate the potential harm a status-quo immigration policy can do to the country's economic fortunes, its international reputation or its very sense of itself.

. . .

This brings me back to the man I met in Calgary, who had decided to leave Canada to return to his country of origin in pursuit of his dream for a better life for his wife and children. In the final analysis, the casualty of a dysfunctional immigration system is not simply the newcomers and their jilted aspirations, but very likely Canadian society itself. Recent immigrants, especially the highly skilled ones that our point system favours, have never had more options than they do today. As the countries from which they emigrated continue to modernize and as foreign governments court members of expatriate communities to return home, the brain drain of Canadian talent and knowledge will be noticeable and felt most acutely within our immigrant populations. The loss of these talented individuals affects not only the business sector and Canada's international competitiveness. By failing to create the preconditions for the kinds of economic and social mobility that could have forged lasting bonds of loyalty between skilled newcomers and their adopted country, Canada risks shedding the very human capital which could have made our aspiration to be the world's immigration exemplar into more than a rhetorical boast.

What worries me most is the impact of a failing immigration and settlement system on the country's self-confidence. This is, after all, one of the last areas of mostly federal jurisdiction where there is overwhelming public support for ambitious policy-making. If we fall into the trap of mythologizing the Canadian immigrant experience in the same way that we have mythologized our contributions to peacekeeping, and if we fail to understand how the larger world is changing, then one of the great and noble social projects that has captivated our collective imagination for almost three decades could all but evaporate.

At this moment in our history, when we have hollowed out so many national institutions, it is far from clear what, if anything, could take the place of immigration as a rallying point to give our society purpose and direction. My hope is that enough of us will realize that the risk of not articulating an inspiring and inclusive vision of Canadian citizenship while at the same time encouraging high levels of immigration is too great. We must recognize that mass immigration has profoundly and irrevocably changed the country and that we have only one course of action: to create real and lasting opportunities for economic and social advancement for recent immigrants, especially visible minorities, and to find ways to bind their futures to Canada's.

5 | FIRST PRINCIPLES

WHEN faced with the litany of domestic and international issues crying out for attention, policy makers and pundits have a standard operating procedure: they try to shake the country out of the habit of ignoring its pressing medium- and long-term challenges by prescribing a stiff tonic of sweeping policy recommendations to put Canada back on track. As well-intentioned and thought-out as these prescriptions may be, they mostly fail to understand that the task at hand is not one of coming up with rafts of policy options to address the problems afflicting the Canadian body politic. Rather, the challenge before us is to advance an overarching idea for the country, an understanding of who we are that is based on the lessons of our history and the convictions that define us as a people. For me, the resilience of our shared nationhood is not just the product of our natural wealth, our dynamic cities or our international accomplishments. The country's larger promise—its potential not just to survive but triumph over the forces that threaten our collective way of life—flows from our storied past and from the immutable beliefs about the nature and purpose of Canadian society that our forebears fought to establish over generations.

If ever there was a period in our history that might be instructive for our own times, it is the early decades of the nineteenth century, in particular the ten years between the Rebellions of 1837 and the achievement of responsible government in 1848. During that time, the colonies of British North America—Upper and Lower Canada, Prince Edward Island, New Brunswick and Nova Scotia— were buffeted by the effects of mass immigration on a scale that dwarfs today's numbers. Colonial society was riven by deep sectarian divisions based on religion, nationality and class. Reminiscent of present-day discussions about the country's core principles, but many times more intense, almost every political and social debate of the day revolved around the question of loyalty. Who could be trusted in the aftermath of America's attempted invasions between 1812 and 1814? Where was the next secessionist plot or insurrection likely to erupt? Which ideas were sedition and who would decide?

This fractured, suspicious, inward-looking colonial community was besieged by forces not unlike those pulling at the fabric of Canadian society today, but on a scale that is difficult for us to comprehend. Yet ten short years after the dark days that followed the Rebellions, a new political order was born, one that successfully united the colonies' disparate elements around a series of simple but powerful ideas about how democracy in British North America should work. This consensus provided the blueprint for Confederation and the democratic values of Canadian society for the next century and a half. It also contained a series of immutable truths about our country that, properly appreciated and understood today, could help us summon for our time a robust civic identity capable of tackling the social, political and economic challenges that lie in our near future.

To understand the story of Canada's evolution as a democracy and its many twists and turns along the way, one has to acknowledge the central role that loyalty plays in our civic culture. The powerful emotion of loyalty—not abstract ideas about individual freedom or the rights of man—is the terra firma of our political history, thanks to one of the world's great revolutions, the American War of Independence.

The tens of thousands of men, women and children who fled the thirteen southern colonies between 1776 and the early 1800s lost everything: their farms, homes, livelihoods and positions in society. Because of their allegiance to the British Crown and Constitution, many suffered the rough justice of revolutionary tribunals, including corporal punishment and public humiliation. For these anti-revolutionaries, the uprising was not a struggle for liberty against high British taxes or any other so-called grievance; it was the work of a small minority of rabble-rousing ringleaders bent on political power and personal profit. The illegal seizure of their properties and businesses, the persecution of religious minorities and the collapse of basic social order that accompanied the insurrection seared into the Loyalist consciousness a deep and abiding distrust of democratic experimentation and the designs of the newly independent American nation.

These sentiments dovetailed perfectly with the world view of the conservative Tory elites who ran the hardscrabble northern colonies. The day-to-day operations of the colonial governments were overseen by a coterie of British army officers, members of the establishment Church of England and a tight-knit group of provincial gentry linked by patronage, marriage and their belief in the executive power of the Governors General appointed by the Crown. Like the Loyalists from the south, the elites of Upper and Lower Canada and the Atlantic colonies viewed the American Revolution as a cautionary tale: the toleration of even modest dissent could spiral into dangerous civil insurrection. For both groups—the country's first generation of anti-Americans—political opposition of any kind was tantamount to disloyalty.

By the end of its war with Britain, the American republic was vastly more powerful economically than the materially under-developed northern colonies. It was starkly evident, too, that its experiment with democracy was succeeding and that its citizens enjoyed a degree of personal freedom and social mobility that far outstripped anything the political culture of British North America was able, or willing, to offer. For the Loyalists and their Tory hosts, the losses and privations suffered in the revolution and its wake had to mean something greater; their sacrifice had to contribute to some larger destiny for British North America, preferably one superior to that of the revolutionary republic to the south. Both Loyalists and established elites seized on their attachment to imperial Britain and the aristocratic elements of its "balanced" Constitution as the source of their inspiration for the more peaceful, lawful and well-ordered society they would now set out to build. According to historian S.F. Wise, "it was essential for Canadians not to believe in the United States and to assume that the country they lived in was not a kind of subarctic, second-best America but rather a genuine alternative to this revolution-born democracy and organized upon principles and for purposes quite different from it."

But there was a fly in the ointment, a possible threat to their dream of British North America as a string of stout Loyalist bastions straddling the northern half of the continent, impervious to the revolutionary temptations of the southern neighbour. The potential spoiler was massive immigration. Attracted by offers of free and verdant land from the colonial governments, unantici-pated numbers of Americans, primarily poor farmers, poured into the British colonies in the late eighteenth and early nine-teenth centuries. Census data indicate that the population of the colonies doubled to 800,000 in the twenty years following the war—the equivalent of present-day Canada absorbing 1.5 million immigrants a year for the next two decades. The reaction of the loyalty-obsessed colonial governments was as swift as it was predictable. Could these immigrants be trusted? They had not proven their loyalty through the fire of revolution, and unlike immigrants from Britain they had been living in a revolutionary society rife with seditious ideas. Might the new settlers, in fact, comprise a fifth column that would rise up against their Tory hosts when an ever more expansionist and militaristic America eventually turned its covetous eyes northwards?

Answering the first question in the negative and the second in the affirmative, the colonies' elites—now made up mostly of Loyalists who had arrived in the direct aftermath of the American Revolution—closed ranks. They systematically excluded the new arrivals from the colonies' governing institutions and from the spoils of patronage, the keys to personal wealth and influence in British North America. The late-arriving Americans were barred from sitting on the legislatures' executive councils, which advised the colonial administration, and were denied even minor government posts and appointments. The titles to the land they had been granted were put into legal limbo, and the path to full citizenship and social acceptance for three-quarters of British North America's inhabitants remained anything but clear. To the Tories, the benefits of full citizenship were not something that could be acquired through a process of assimilation, that is, by living in the society and contributing to its civic and economic enrichment. Only those who were from "good Loyalist stock" or who had proven their devotion to king and country at bayonet point could aspire to leadership and power.

If the outlines of a distinctly Canadian political culture gelled first around issues of loyalty during the American Revolution, then it is fair to say that unquestioning allegiance to the colonial administration was the supreme civic virtue during the War of 1812. The American invasion confirmed the worst fears of the colonies' ruling class concerning the warlike nature of revolutionary societies and stiffened their determination that British North America should be a counter-revolutionary project, resolutely opposed, as arch-conservative John Strachan put it, to the "licentiousness of the people." Happily, the eventual victory of the colonies' armies over large and well-equipped American forces at Chateauguay, Crysler's Farm and the bloody battle of Lundy's Lane served to bolster the Loyalist myth that unity and obedience to the existing social order were the fathers of their success—and the bedrock of their social and political life.

The fealty of all but a handful of American immigrants residing in what is now Ontario, Quebec and the Maritimes earned these recent arrivals no credit whatsoever. Indeed, during the war, rumours swirled that American settlers had organized armed insurrections and only the miraculous defeat of the American forces had saved the colonies from open revolt. In the words of the British general and hero of the War of 1812, Sir Isaac Brock, "There can be no doubt that a large portion of the population...are either indifferent to what is passing, or so completely American as to rejoice in the prospects of a change in Government."

Fear of possible American invasions in the future and mistrust of the existing immigrant population prompted colonial governments in the 1820s to curtail immigration from the United States in favour of "loyal" newcomers from Britain. They continued to deny post-revolution settlers of non-British origin the status of legal subjects, including in some cases the right to vote or to own property. As one arch-Tory vowed at the time, he and his kind would "suffer death before...conferring the rights of a subject on men who, but a few years ago, had invaded our country—ransacked our villages—burnt our houses—and murdered our wives and children."

The Tory elites' arbitrary and unjust assault on these colonists' basic rights galvanized for the first time the nascent reformist elements in Upper Canada. The early Reformers were mostly prosperous farmers and members of the growing professional classes—lawyers, doctors and shopkeepers—frustrated with the self-dealing of the colonial governments and the rigid political control exercised by the Governors General. All immigrants themselves, they believed the large number of newcomers settling in the colonies after the War of 1812, especially those from America, could be absorbed into society as productive and faithful citizens—just as they and their families had been in the aftermath of the American Revolution. In their view, full citizenship and its attendant privileges could be earned by immigrants through contributing to the colony's economic welfare, schooling their children and responsibly exercising their political freedoms.

Such arguments for an assimilative and participatory model of citizenship resonate with our twenty-first-century sensibilities. In these first difficult debates about the essence of citizenship, English-speaking Canada began to develop its own national consciousness. For the reform-minded minority, the strength of their society rested not on the preservation of an ethnic British bloodline or on an attitude of blind obedience to the colonial administration. Rather, the colony's innate natural abundance and economic potential, combined with the British Constitution's protection of individual liberty and property rights, could make loyal citizens of every newcomer. In other words, the colonists' sense of shared identity and purpose was based on loyalty not only to the British Crown and its institutions, but increasingly to the realities of life in the colonies: the physical land, the sense of community, the greater social mobility and the economic opportunities that the colonies of British North America afforded newcomers. This sentiment comes through in an anonymous contemporary letter to the editor: "Another half century will make [the American settlers'] children Canadians, at all events; and all distinction of country will then be forgotten."

The great citizenship debate in Upper Canada was ultimately resolved to the satisfaction of the Reformers and the American immigrants when in 1828 the Colonial Office in Britain forced the colony's administrators to naturalize all immigrants who had settled before 1820. This reversal, however, ended up hardening the attitudes of the Tory governing class. Their attempts to entrench an exclusive and exclusionary citizenship had failed, and now they faced an organized opposition which had just tasted its first political victory. Conflict seemed all but inevitable as colonial governments held to the line that all political dissent was disloyal and that to entertain the reform of the colony's democratic institutions was to show weakness in the face of an enemy within, one bent on fomenting rebellion as the precursor to a second invasion.

WITH A REBEL YELL

According to Mark Twain, while "History does not repeat itself…it does rhyme." The resistance of the colonial elites to granting new arrivals and the pre-existing French majority full participation in British North America's political and economic life ultimately triggered the very upheaval they had so desperately wanted to avoid. In Upper and Lower Canada and in the Maritimes, the catalyst was not punitive taxation or the meddling of the motherland in domestic affairs, as it had been in the War of Independence. The colonists' attachment to the imperial connection had remained strong after that war, even in Quebec where religious and legal protections had been guaranteed and where the French-speaking majority was granted some say in the governance of Lower Canada through the colony's Legislative Assembly. Instead, the armed insurrections that shook British North America in the late 1830s originated with the widening sectarian divisions that mass immigration had introduced to the colonies.

Contrary to popular belief, Canada was a culturally heterogeneous country long before waves of post–Second World War migrants changed the ethnic composition of Canadian society in the second half of the last century. The period of greatest sustained immigration to Canada began in the 1820s and continued for more than fifty years. Then, as now, mass immigration fundamentally transformed the culture and political dynamics of the colonies. During the two short decades that separated the War of 1812–14 from the Rebellions of 1837, British North America went from being an ethnically homogenous and cohesive entity— acknowledging the exception of the existing French habitants and Aboriginal population—to a society sharply divided on sectarian lines. Along with large numbers of newcomers from Britain (encouraged by the Tory elites to ensure the colonial populations remained loyal to the Crown) and the steady flow of economic migrants from America came not just the dreams of a better life in the New World but also the religious and cultural prejudices of the Old.

As record numbers of impoverished Irish Catholics and Scottish Protestants flooded Atlantic Canada, Montreal and present-day southern Ontario, an already testy colonial political culture became ethnically polarized. In Lower Canada, the Protestants lent their muscle to the ruling anglophone aristocracy in return for patronage and social acceptance whereas for reasons of religion the Irish Catholics aligned themselves with the French Catholic majority. In Upper Canada, the Irish Catholics and likewise poor American immigrants were inclined to side with the

Reformers and take up the call for land reform, especially the development of the extensive and dormant tracts set aside by the Constitution Act of 1791 for the Anglican Church. Irish Protestants, in contrast, established branches of Ireland's infamous Orange Order and provided the colonial government with an informal militia to help intimidate the burgeoning Reform movement at the local level.

Historian Desmond Morton dates the beginnings of the Canadian habit of co-opting immigrants into ideological battles to this tumultuous period: "Irish Canadians provided the test-bed for Canada's long tradition of ethnic politics, from pandering to the fears of disdainful or suspicious neighbours to cultivation of leaders and subsidization of ethnic media in return for bloc followings." Sectarian tensions were at their worst in Atlantic Canada, where, in the 1820s and 1830s, violent riots between Catholics and Protestants broke out regularly.

Alongside these divides there developed resentments between the more recent, poorer arrivals, or "pauper immigrants," as they were called, and longer-settled groups. This was especially so in Quebec, where newer British and American immigrants were seen as part of a concerted strategy to dilute the French majority. In Ontario and the Maritimes, anti-immigrant sentiment also ran high as colonial economies remained stagnant compared with the booming growth south of the border. The competition for good land was fierce, and the sudden surplus of cheap labour in the cities and towns was a hardship for newcomers and longer-settled colonists alike, the latter still being frozen out of patronage appointments to government jobs.

By the 1830s, the major conflicts in Upper Canada and the Atlantic colonies arose not from the competing definitions of loyalty held by Reformers and Tories, but from the frustrated economic and political ambitions of new immigrants. Endemic corruption among the tiny circle of colonial administrators and the awarding of land and lucrative government posts to government supporters rankled the latest British-born immigrants as much as the American settlers. They saw few opportunities for advancement, despite the professional skills they had to offer, and the exclusionary model of citizenship cherished by the Tories was unable to claim their affections, let alone their allegiance. The exceptions were the Irish Protestants who, faithful to the causes of their homeland, enthusiastically joined in stamping out dissent against the established Protestant church and government.

In Lower Canada, the catalysts for rebellion were similar but distinct. The grievances of the French-speaking majority were the same as those elsewhere: the unchecked executive powers of the colonial governors, the abuse of patronage to reward and entrench a governing anglophone elite and absentee landlords who exploited struggling farmers. Like the other colonies, Lower Canada had, by the 1830s, experienced a growth in its middle class; professionals such as doctors and lawyers and the sons of wealthy French landowners wanted a greater role in the colony's government and administration. But their ambitions were blocked by a Constitution that vested power in a legislative council and judiciary appointed by the colonial governor. The French dominated the Legislative Assembly, but it was effectively toothless. So, too, with political patronage. In Lower Canada, government appointments were distributed according to ethnic and class affiliation and *les Canadiens* were all but excluded. Just as the English colonies' growing professional class was attracted to the Reform movement, the rising bourgeoisie of Lower Canada flocked to the new Patriote Party and the charismatic Louis-Joseph Papineau.

However, the effect of mass immigration on colonial politics in Lower Canada was somewhat different. Starting in the 1830s, the significant increase in British and American newcomers settling around Montreal became a pressing concern for the French majority. If they lost their numerical dominance, especially in the colony's legislature, the colonial government might use a large British immigrant voting block to dismantle the laws, institutions and language protections that had ensured the survival of the Québécois since the Conquest. Historian Allan Greer points out that "a substantial majority of adult males could vote, and this fact implies a degree of democracy that would have been unheard of in Britain, in most of the United States, and even in revolutionary France...the habitants, because they outnumbered all other classes combined, held the key to every election."

During elections in the 1830s, the clashes between Patriote demonstrators and Protestant supporters of candidates loyal to the colonial governor further impressed on the Québécois the threat that British immigration posed to their control of the colony's Legislative Assembly. As the 1830s drew to a close, poor harvests, worsening sectarian violence and an intransigent colonial governor made the "troubles" that soon swept through Lower Canada all but inevitable.

As it turned out, both rebellions were miserable failures. In Upper Canada, the march down Toronto's Yonge Street of a couple of hundred ragtag radical Reformers behind firebrand William Lyon Mackenzie could, in the words of one historian, "best be described as a farce, but for the loss of life." Two rebels were shot dead by the militia, and the leaders of the short-lived uprising fled across the border into New York state. Two more rebels where caught and later tried and executed. Throughout the colony, Reformers were rounded up by militias constituted from the Orange Lodges. The majority of these supposed revolutionaries had had nothing to do with the rebellion. Anyone with political influence who had exhibited reform sympathies was hounded out of public office and ostracized.

Events in Lower Canada were far more serious. When the British parliament passed legislation allowing the colony's governor to spend public money without the approval of the Legislative Assembly—thereby abolishing the one substantive constitutional lever held by the French-dominated lower house—mass protests broke out across the colony. Violent confrontations between the protesters and mostly Protestant immigrant militias enflamed thousands of Patriotes in towns outside of Montreal to take up arms against the government. After a successful first skirmish at Saint-Denis, the lightly armed rebel troops gathered at Saint-Charles, Saint-Eustache and in surrounding hamlets, where they were mercilessly attacked by regular forces of the British army.

A second, larger uprising the following winter was also crushed by the better-equipped-and-organized British army. Patriote villages that had sheltered the rebels or put up a fight were torched and looted by army regulars and the militia. The leaders of the rebellions, mostly young professionals, were arrested and, contrary to British common law, denied trial by jury. The subsequent military courts martial were presided over by the same officers who had put down the rebellions. Of the 111 men charged with high treason, twelve were hung and another fifty-eight were deemed to be "dangerous characters" and sentenced to life terms in Australia's penal colonies. In all, some three hundred Patriotes died in the two campaigns.

DEMOCRACY'S DECADE

Although the rebellions had failed, the Tory establishment's concept of loyalty was exposed for what it was: an outmoded notion of privilege deeply at odds with the emerging national and democratic spirit of the colonies. The state-sanctioned repression that followed the rebellions, much of which was overtly sectarian, represented a fundamental crisis. What would happen to British North America if the fealty of the colonists could not be won by the Loyalist example of sacrifice and faith in the social hierarchy, and instead could only be achieved by the force of arms? How would the all-important connection with Britain be maintained, and with it a destiny separate from America, if the colonies' governing institutions lacked even the semblance of popular legitimacy? And if neither the old Tory model of loyalty nor the rebel's cry for republican government were able to hold the fractious colonies together, then what new civic culture could unite and inspire an emerging Canadian nation?

Three men, one a member of a prominent Irish political family in Ontario, one a former Patriote leader and the third a fiery newspaper publisher in Nova Scotia, took it upon themselves to find answers to these questions. In doing so, they redefined in the 1840s the nature of civic loyalty and thereby established the ethical foundations of our modern-day democracy.

Robert Baldwin was a Reform movement moderate and Upper Canada's most eloquent and senior spokesman for the cause of responsible government—the idea that the colonies should be governed by a cabinet answerable to an elected legislature, not by the executive fiat of a Governor General. Because he had tried to negotiate the stand-down of Mackenzie's followers at Montgomery's Tavern on the eve of the rebellion, Baldwin was falsely accused by his Tory opponents as a rebel. His principled advocacy for responsible government during the two previous decades was publicly discredited by the charge that he had helped foment the revolt, and his family was financially ruined.

Louis-Hippolyte LaFontaine was a member of the Lower Canada Assembly who emerged as the undisputed political leader of French Canada in the rebellion's aftermath. A moderate like Baldwin, he thought the uprisings were a tragic mistake. When the first skirmishes broke out, he defied both the rebel leadership and the colonial administration to travel to Britain to plead for the reopening of the Legislative Assembly and the establishment of responsible government. For his efforts, he was briefly imprisoned on his return to Lower Canada on a trumped-up sedition charge.

Rebuilding the Reform movement during a period of resurgent Toryism following the rebellions was difficult enough, but both leaders soon had to also deal with the fallout of the British government's official report on the 1837–38 uprisings. Lord Durham's famous conclusion that the root of the colonies' problems flowed from the fact that there were "two nations warring within the bosom of a single state" prompted the Colonial Office to merge Upper and Lower Canada into a single political unit, the Province of Canada, with a single parliament. The goal of what in 1840 was called the Act of Union was the assimilation of French Canada. To quote Lord Durham, "The union of the two provinces would not only give a clear English majority, but one which would be increased every year by the influence of English emigration; and I have little doubt that the French, when once placed, by the legitimate course of events and the working of natural causes, in a minority, would abandon their vain hopes of nationality."

A more immediate objective of the union was the dilution of the Reform elements in both provinces in a Parliament in which the Protestant English minority in Quebec would combine with the Tory elements in Upper Canada to form a powerful conservative majority in support of the status quo. The use of French was banned in the new legislature and wholesale political patronage was used to plant opponents of responsible government in key administrative positions. During elections for the combined Parliament, the colonial administration unleashed the Protestant Orange Order on Reform candidates in English Canada and stoked sectarian divisions to dampen the Reform vote in present-day Quebec. LaFontaine himself ended up losing his seat when the polling station where his supporters were supposed to cast their ballots was barricaded by hundreds of club-wielding Tory toughs.

How did LaFontaine and Baldwin react to these setbacks, which followed so quickly on the humiliations of 1837–38? Both understood that the path to democracy lay in a policy of active collaboration between francophone and anglophone reformers, not in rebellion. They decided to exploit the democratic potential of the new assembly to form a powerful French-English Reform majority and promote a new idea of loyalty. This non-sectarian alliance would win legitimacy in the eyes of the people and peacefully take power from the executive by championing policies and ideas that gave expression to an emerging Canadian national identity. As Robert Baldwin said, "I...wish to see a provincial [as opposed to a British] feeling pervade the whole mass of our population...to see every man belong to us proud of the Canadian name, and of Canada as his country."

It was Baldwin who took the first crucial steps to put the Reform agenda into action. When the Governor General failed to heed his advice that Reformers, including LaFontaine, should be appointed to the Executive Council, Baldwin resigned from the government on the grounds that the principle of responsibility had been violated. Next, he arranged for LaFontaine to run in a by-election in one of the two Toronto-area ridings that had previously elected him to Parliament. The Catholic leader of French Canada was triumphantly returned to the legislature by a mainly Protestant, Upper Canadian constituency. This extraordinary gesture cemented the French-English Reform partnership.

The hands-on task of making responsible government politically respectable fell to LaFontaine. In English Canada, this would be no small feat: the Loyalist instinct was to regard any reduction in the power of the Governor General as a weakening of the imperial connection upon which the colony's future existence was thought to depend. In French Canada, his challenge must have seemed near impossible. For the Québécois, the Act of Union meant the loss of the legislative majority they had enjoyed in the Lower Canada Assembly, a majority they had used for half a century to protect their laws, institutions and language. In the combined Parliament, their fate rested with a numerically equivalent but faster growing English Protestant population.

LaFontaine's genius was to understand how to bridge these two constituencies. By advancing a political platform that encouraged economic development, land reform, the more equitable distribution of patronage, public education and stronger local government, LaFontaine appealed to the ambitions of the rising commercial immigrant class in English Canada, men such as the young John A. Macdonald. He was able to bring French Canadians into his coalition in droves, despite the best efforts of a radical republican movement, the Parti Rouge, which was formed in response to the Act of Union and sought annexation by America. Rebel or not, all French Canadians wanted an end to the Tory establishment's vise-like grip on patronage in Montreal. They were willing to lend their votes to the alliance with English reformers, provided the French language and religious minority rights were respected and both groups shared in government appointments and contracts.

The new bond of loyalty that united these historically disparate, if not antagonistic, groups still had a British complexion, namely their allegiance to responsible government and the personal liberty afforded by the British Constitution. But in its scope and character, it was uniquely Canadian, an expression of the realities of the previous fifty years of colonial history, but also a harbinger of Canada's bicultural future.

In the Atlantic colonies, similar hard-fought battles were waged throughout the 1840s between Reform-dominated legislatures and a string of obstinate Governors General. The leading advocate for responsible government in the Maritimes was the mercurial Joseph Howe. In Nova Scotia, he stood at the head of a powerful Reform movement whose base of support among Protestant immigrants allowed him to control the Legislative Assembly. But Howe and his supporters faced the same problem that bedevilled the Province of Canada: the unwillingness of successive Governors General to allow the majority party in the legislature to form the executive council out of their own party members. Citing concerns about sectarian divisions, the governors pursued a policy of "non-partisan" responsible government under which both Tories and Reformers were asked to join the executive council, regardless of their representation in the Assembly.

Howe, like LaFontaine, created a coalition that could bridge sectarian divides and win the support of the emerging middle class. But unlike LaFontaine, Howe left politics in the middle of Nova Scotia's struggle for responsible government when he resigned in protest against the Governor General's arbitrary use of political patronage. In 1844, he returned to journalism and launched a vociferous public campaign against the colonial administration and the Tory-led executive. In a series of landmark editorials, he set out a detailed Reform agenda of public education, local government, land reform, public infrastructure development, the end of denominational schools and an expansion of the voting franchise.

Thanks to the power of Howe's pen, when the Reformers won a majority in the Assembly in 1847, with strong Catholic as well as Protestant support, the then-Governor General allowed the victors to select the executive council from among their own members. The legislature that sat in January 1848 was Canada's first truly responsible government; Howe returned to serve as provincial secretary. The remaining three Atlantic provinces would follow Nova Scotia's example, but not until the middle of the next decade.

Three months later, on March 9, 1848, democracy came to the Province of Canada in name, if not in spirit. LaFontaine and Baldwin had won a majority of seats in Parliament and were asked to form a government. To do so, they selected a cabinet, for the first time, from among their own elected members. LaFontaine was named government leader. This was the moment when responsible government was formally achieved in the Province of Canada, the constitutional conclusion of a decade of parliamentary struggle between Tories, Reformers and the Governors General. But real, working democracy did not arrive until almost a year later, in a far more dramatic fashion.

The opposition formed almost immediately after LaFontaine and Baldwin's victory. For the Tory ruling class and Orange Order Protestants, having a French Canadian and former Patriote elected as government leader and the Reform-friendly Lord Elgin installed as Governor General was a bitter pill. So, too, was losing the perks that came with controlling the public purse and political patronage. But what was absolutely unacceptable to the old regime was Parliament's passage of legislation compensating the former residents of Lower Canada for their losses and damage to property during the rebellions.

Despite similar compensation to property owners in Upper Canada, the Montreal Tories in particular saw the Rebellion Losses Bill as an act of treason. In the eyes of the government's critics, LaFontaine had created an upside-down world where, instead of the Loyalist being venerated for his allegiance to Britain and the Crown, the rebel was rewarded for his sedition and treachery. For Tories, the bill undid half a century of colonial history and discarded the hard-fought-for identity of British North America as a Loyalist bastion.

In the weeks following the bill's passage, hundreds and then thousands of protesters took to the streets in Toronto and Montreal. Effigies of LaFontaine and Baldwin burned, and thousands signed petitions demanding that the Governor General stop the bill. The Tory press fed the mood of crisis: "Men of Canada of British origin, no sleep to the eyes, no slumber to the eyelids, until you have avenged this most atrocious, this most unparalleled insult!"

But despite the threat of civil unrest and mounting pressure from the British press and Tory politicians in England to disallow the legislation, Lord Elgin quietly gave the bill his assent. The principle of responsible government—the tenet that the executive was bound to follow the advice of ministers who had the confidence of the Legislative Assembly—was upheld.

When news of the Governor General's decision spread through Montreal, angry mobs gathered in the streets. Soon a group of two thousand or more outraged Tories and their supporters massed on Montreal's Champ de Mars. After a series of incendiary speeches, the cry went up, "To the Parliament House!" The Assembly building, where members were sitting late into the night, was surrounded and its windows smashed by a volley of stones before rioters stormed the entrance. The hall was destroyed in minutes and set alight. The entire structure, including a library of 20,000 volumes, was engulfed in flames, illuminating the city from the mountain to the river. In the days after, anarchy reigned in the streets of Montreal. LaFontaine's house was sacked and burned, various Reform printing presses destroyed and the Governor General's carriage attacked. Finally, the army and a thousand special constables patrolling the streets restored a semblance of order.

This attack on Canada's fledgling democracy was one of the great turning points in Canadian history. As John Ralston Saul noted, "The government's response would cause this place either to slip down the European/American road towards impossible oppositions, outright violence and a centralized monolithic model. Or the ministers would have to discover another way." The immediate danger was that the Governor General and the Colonial Office would capitulate to pressure from Britain and the threat of more violence in Canada and repeal the Rebellion Losses Bill. LaFontaine and the French Reformers also had to decide what their response would be to the burning of Parliament and to the attacks on persons and property. Should Tory mob violence be met with a similar Reform reaction on the streets of Montreal and Toronto? Now that the Reformers had control of government, it was well within their prerogative to push for courts martial and capital punishment for the mob's leaders—the same punitive justice that had been meted out to the rebels of 1837. And even if some kind of compromise could be reached on the Rebellion Losses Bill, what would stop the Orange Order and Tory agitators from resorting to civil strife in the future to thwart the democratic will of the Assembly?

It is no exaggeration to suggest that the province's very identity hung in the balance during those fateful weeks. The colony's politics could either return to the old divisions of ethnicity and class—French versus English, Protestant versus Catholic and Reform versus Tory—or the Reform movement that had gathered steam over the previous decade could prevail and Canadian society would finally start to free itself of its sectarian shackles.

The crisis was averted by LaFontaine and Elgin correctly reading the public's mood. Both the elected government and the colonial administration did nothing. The bill stood as passed. The troops remained in their barracks. The mob's leaders were not prosecuted. In effect, the Tory opposition was quieted into an uneasy submission by the stark contrast between their outpouring of violence and the calm and orderly efforts of the Reformers to return the colony to normalcy.

In the weeks and months that followed, responsible government became more than political theory. Its wide acceptance and the public's rejection of mob violence demonstrated how far Canadians had come in terms of their understanding of the meaning and nature of loyalty. Canadians were for the first time in their history loyal to themselves—to institutions and civic values that had been created out of the unique historical, cultural and political forces that had shaped British North America since the War of 1812.

With the Reform Losses Bill behind them, LaFontaine and Baldwin set about implementing their Reform agenda in the three-year period that historians would later call the "Great Ministry." The last of the rebels still being held in penal colonies were pardoned and allowed to return home. The decades-long fight over the relationship of the Anglican Church to higher education was brought to an end with the passage of legislation that established the University of Toronto as a publicly funded, non-sectarian institution. Baldwin took a hand in bringing to a successful conclusion the struggle for local self-government that had paralleled the fight for parliamentary reform. The offices of governor-appointed justices of the peace, who had once directed the management of local affairs and assessed local taxes, were abolished. In their place, townships were created as independently incorporated bodies run by locally elected officials. These new municipalities had the ability to levy taxes as they saw fit and, more importantly, spend those monies according to local direction on schools, roads and the general infrastructure. In total, close to two hundred pieces of legislation were enacted, covering everything from judicial reform to government investment in railway and canal systems to the first attempt to strike a free-trade agreement with the United States.

During this same period, Joseph Howe was implementing an almost identical reform agenda in Nova Scotia. New investments were made in communications, including improving the Post Office and telegraph systems, the judiciary was modernized along with the public service and vast tracks of fallow land previously granted to the church and absentee landlords were prepared for settlement by immigrants. Howe personally took on the Herculean task of reforming the public education system along non-denominational lines. He also initiated an almost ten-year battle to build a publicly owned railway system to stimulate commerce within the province and ultimately link Nova Scotia's economy with the economies of central Canada and the vast western interior.

LESSONS LEARNED

Just as significant as this incredible onslaught of legislation was the spirit in which it was conceived and implemented. Behind all of these reforms lay a vision of Canada as an egalitarian, democratic, economically ambitious and less sectarian society—concepts that would have been unconceivable ten short years earlier in the Rebellions' aftermath. Stephen Leacock describes this period as the time when the "forces of racial antipathy, separation and rebellion, scarce checked by the union of 1840, pass into that broader movement which makes towards confederation and the creation of a continental Dominion."

Again, what is crucial to understand about this chapter in Canada's history is how our perceptions of what one should be loyal to, and why, changed. The transformations between 1812 and 1848 were multiple and remarkable. To start, the focus of loyalty shifted from the Governors General and the imperial connection to the democratic legislatures and to power-sharing between the long-settled French minority and the growing English immigrant majority—all at the expense of the Tory elite. In addition, the historical narrative that had underpinned the colonial societies' sense of identity moved from the American Revolution and the War of 1812's "barracks mentality" to the Reformers' ennobling struggle for responsible government and Canada's future as a bicultural nation.

And, perhaps most importantly, our notions of civic virtue and shared citizenship were transformed. Canadians no longer had to demonstrate a feudal-like allegiance to their immediate national and religious group: British or French, Catholic or Protestant. Instead, it became legitimate for our deepest loyalties to encompass our democratic legislatures and local governments and the opportunities for self-government that both offered each colonist, regardless of language or religious creed. The unshackling of our definitions of loyalty saw us embrace a model of citizenship that allowed full membership in the colonies' political and social life to be earned through the act of settlement and nation building as opposed to it being a reward conferred, or not, by the colonial administration.

In effect, with the attainment of responsible government in 1848, the debate about who Canadians were to be loyal to and why—a debate that had begun with the Boston Tea Party and consumed the colonies for three-quarters of a century—came to an end. Although new secessionist and sectarian movements emerged in the 1850s, the reality was that after the "Great Ministry" there would be no "alternative futures" for British North America. Instead, the country would evolve in accordance with a shared adherence to British democratic institutions and indigenous civic traditions that sought to protect important minority rights while advancing individual liberty. American-style democracy, outright secession or a return to the aristocratic rule of the Governors General and the colonial elites were all political dead ends.

This chapter in our history illustrates the fact that a powerful civic nationalism was flourishing in Canada in the twenty years before Confederation and almost a century and a half prior to the Charter of Rights and Freedoms and official multiculturalism. It brought French and English, Protestants and Catholics, and Loyalist, American and British-born immigrants together around the common cause of political reform. It made the very notion of political dissent legitimate in a counter-revolutionary society that lived under the constant threat of invasion by an openly expansionist neighbour. It endured two armed revolts and their polarizing aftermaths, one of which was a genuinely popular uprising. It assimilated unprecedented numbers of immigrants, many of whom brought with them the ancient animosities of their homelands. And it unleashed a flurry of nation building, everything from non-denominational schooling to effective local government to new railways, canals and the telegraph. In short, our forebears called forth and institutionalized, in the space of a generation, a common civic creed that refashioned British North America into a democratic society built on bicultural principles of self-government, along increasingly non-sectarian lines.

6 | CANADA FOUND—AND LOST

AMONG the most rewarding initiatives undertaken by the Dominion Institute is the Memory Project, a program that has helped some 3,000 veterans visit with almost one million school children since 2001. Battling the infirmities of age and burdened by painful memories of wars fought more than sixty years ago, these men and women offer young people—as no textbook or Hollywood movie ever could—a first-hand lesson about the awesome responsibilities of citizenship. They possess a quiet confidence and are tireless when it comes to giving back to their local communities; their optimism about the country and its future prospects is steadfast.

The fearlessness of Canada's "greatest generation" is also striking. I once spoke with a survivor of the Dieppe Raid who described to me in the starkest terms what it was like landing on the French coast on that August morning in 1942 and making his way up the pebbled beach under relentless machine-gun fire. As his mates fell around him, wounded or dying, he suddenly heard a tremendous "bam" and fell to the ground, stunned. His first thought was that a German artillery shell had barely missed him. Then he felt blood streaming down his neck and chest and realized he was seriously wounded in the face. The experience of being shot and having to wait, slipping in and out of consciousness, until he was captured by German troops was so terrifying that after the war he found that nothing in his life ever truly frightened him again. I heard the same sentiments expressed by men whose airplanes had disintegrated around them in a hail of enemy fire, by soldiers who had endured months of infantry combat and by prisoners of war who had suffered years of mind-numbing captivity and physical privation.

The return to civilian life of most of the 1.1 million Canadians who served in uniform in the Second World War—an extraordinary number from a country whose population in 1945 totaled only 11 million—had far-reaching effects on the national psyche. The sacrifice of 42,000 combat deaths and another 52,000 wounded had to count for something greater than the victory itself. The combined effects of the war and of the Depression a decade earlier made it unacceptable that Canada should slip back into a pre-war social order where average Canadians were expected to sink or swim on their own.

Equally, Canada's outstanding war record raised expectations about the country's stature internationally. With the third largest navy and fourth largest air force, new industrial capacity, vital mineral resources—including the fuel of the coming nuclear age, high grade uranium—and a major role in the reconstruction of Europe, Canadians were ready to step onto the world stage as citizens of an independent nation with its own capabilities and its own interests.

Veterans in particular held attitudes about the country in 1945 that were quite different from those of the previous generation at the end of the First World War. Britain could no longer claim the unflinching allegiance of English-speaking Canadians. There would be no equivalents of the annual Vimy anniversary dinners that filled community halls after the Great War, nor pilgrimages of thousands of veterans to European battlefields. The vast majority of Canadians who fought in the Second World War were Canadian-born, and their loyalty was to the country to which they had returned. Furthermore, "imperial" Britain, with its far-flung colonies, military might and financial prowess, had been swept away by the war. The allure of being the senior dominion within the British Empire had faded.

At the same time, while everyone acknowledged the United States' economic and military pre-eminence at war's end, American power did not overwhelm Canadians' sense of pride or faith in their own potential. Historian Frank Underhill may have described Canada's immediate postwar mood best when he wrote, "We are now out in the world on our own. We English-Canadians can no longer, when we try to distinguish ourselves from the Americans, announce that we are British. Somehow or other we have to put a distinctive meaning into the declaration that we are Canadians."

This was the challenge and the opportunity: to formulate a North American identity for the country that simultaneously asserted our autonomy from Britain, our independence from America and our special relationship with both countries. At the same time, that identity had to embrace the country's regions—including Quebec, which had been shaken by a second conscription crisis—and help assimilate an expected flood of immigrants into a new concept of Canadian nationhood.

The story of how Canada reasserted itself in the aftermath of the Second World War represents to me the second great imagining of who we are as a people. Just as in the years after the attainment of responsible government in 1848, the decade following the war saw Canada's political leaders embark on an ambitious program of nation building. With foresight and tenacity, they created a series of institutions which were purpose-built to act as the vehicles of a modern and uniquely Canadian identity. Some of these institutions reinforced the cornerstones of the Reform project a century earlier; others represented a radical departure from the past. But their overall objective was the same: to use the power of collective institutions to assert a national identity capable of bridging the country's internal divisions and articulating a vision for the country, at home and abroad, that was of our own making, an expression of our own values and interests.

A NATION OF INSTITUTIONS

From the vantage point of 2009, it is tempting to portray the Canada of the 1950s as an uncomplicated scene out of *Father Knows Best*. In fact, then, as in the last ten years, the country experienced a period of rapid economic growth. Waves of immigrants from war-ravaged central and southern Europe contributed a new social diversity that enlivened the country. The first suburbs bloomed in widening circles around city cores. The forerunners of universal health care and the social programs that we hold up today as defining features of the country were put into place. Canada's membership in NATO and the notion of peacekeeping—which to this day dominate debates about Canada's role in the world—took shape. Indeed, so much of present-day Canada is rooted in this decade that an aura of historical inevitability hovers over the 1950s and its many milestones.

Overlooked in the clapboard-and-white-picket-fence image of postwar Canada are the deliberate decisions of its political leaders to refashion the country. The modern nation that emerged at the end of the 1950s was not simply the product of a postwar boom; it was, at its heart, the result of a conscious act of will undertaken by a remarkable group of politicians and public servants who struggled against inertia and indifference to redefine Canada's purpose in the twentieth century.

Among them were Louis St. Laurent, the Quebec lawyer and federal justice minister who became prime minister in 1948 and whose avuncular public persona concealed a razor-sharp intellect; C.D. Howe, a businessman-politician who retooled the country's economy during the war; and Lester B. Pearson, the former academic who was St. Laurent's minister of external affairs and later Canada's fourteenth prime minister. Others, such as Norman Robertson and Hume Wrong, the architects of NATO, Brooke Claxton, who championed Canadian culture and the founding of the Canada Council, and Paul Martin Sr., who introduced major health care reforms, are less familiar today, but no less important.

For all of these men, the war was a formative experience. Serving in different capacities inside and outside of government, they witnessed up close the effectiveness of a centralized and dynamic national government. The demands of the war and the enormous problems it posed—reviving a moribund economy, building a battle-ready army, navy and air force, freely supplying billions of dollars in equipment and goods to Britain and the other Allies—forced the country to think big in ways it had not done since the Great War or even the construction of the Canadian Pacific Railway seventy years earlier. As historian Robert Bothwell describes it, "The war had accustomed many Canadians to thinking in national terms. Large problems, such as unemployment, must be solved on a large scale, and the largest Canadian dimension was the dominion government."

The war, in fact, had left more than a couple of extra screwdrivers and wrenches in the Dominion's toolbox. In 1945, Ottawa employed more than 100,000 civil servants, double the number of 1939. The gross national product surged to almost $12 billion in 1945, an 80 percent increase over 1939 levels. This meant that not only were Canadians doing better individually but, thanks to corporate and personal taxes, the government's coffers were considerably fuller than at any time in Canada's past.

Beyond knowing how to read a balance sheet and an organization chart, this generation of seasoned leaders respected the value of effective national institutions. Centralization was not simply about capturing and then keeping certain powers and programs out of the hands of the provinces. What Canada had accomplished during the war, overseas and at home, demonstrated that through economies of scale and centralized planning, the federal government could create new national programs that would meet urgent social and economic needs while at the same time substantiating the country's growing nationalist mood.

Social reform was one of the St. Laurent government's early priorities, a way of directing Canada's new-found prosperity to broader purposes. Although buying a car and a newfangled television set and moving to the suburbs soon became a postwar rite of passage for tens of thousands of Canadians, memories of the poverty and hardship of the Depression years still lingered. In the words of historian William Kilbourn, "The Great Depression of the thirties had never really ended but had rather been absorbed into the war effort. Few Canadians could escape the nagging fear that in peacetime it would inevitably return."

The time was ripe to update basic social services, especially for the poor and vulnerable, and the government began with pension reform. Old-age pensions had been in place since the late 1920s, but only for those seventy years of age and older who were prepared to declare their neediness publicly and submit to a humiliating means test. The new pension plan provided a monthly stipend to every resident seventy and older, and means-tested support to those sixty-five to sixty-nine years of age. Broad public approval ensured that the provinces agreed to a limited constitutional amendment that allowed Ottawa to act in what had previously been an area of exclusive provincial jurisdiction.

Regarding this and other items related to the federal government's social agenda, Ottawa purposely intruded on the constitutional powers of the provinces to advance the national interest. Specifically, the federal government offered to pay for a portion of each new national program; if an individual premier wanted to opt out on constitutional or ideological grounds, then he would have to deal with the ire of his voters come election day. This dynamic was front and centre in the campaign to create a national system of health care insurance, the forerunner to Medicare.

Tommy Douglas had established the first universal hospital care insurance plan in Saskatchewan in 1947 to, in his words, "provide health care for every man, woman and child, regardless of race, colour or financial status." Douglas's insurance scheme was far more expensive than anticipated, however, and the chaos associated with the adoption of a similar program in British Columbia a year later made Ottawa and the other provinces wary about the cost and complexity of introducing a nationwide plan. However, when Ontario agreed to support a national scheme in 1955, the federal government was spurred to action. The resulting legislation, spearheaded by Paul Martin Sr., committed the federal government to paying for half the cost of each provincial plan in operation. After lengthy negotiations with the provinces, the Hospital Insurance and Diagnostic Services Act was finally passed unanimously by Parliament in 1957, with eight provinces on board. Overwhelming public support ensured that all provinces adopted public, universal hospital insurance plans within the next few years.

These universal hospital and old-age pension plans, along with major new federal investments in housing and higher education, made federal-provincial relations prickly throughout the decade. The fiscal underpinnings of federalism—that is, the tax arrangements between the federal and provincial governments—were up for grabs in the 1950s, and with it the balance of power in postwar Canada. The most vocal and obstinate of the provincial leaders were Quebec's Maurice Duplessis and Ontario's George Drew, who argued against the federal government's continuation of the temporary wartime arrangement whereby Ottawa collected all personal and corporate taxes and then made annual payments or grants to the provinces. Duplessis, Drew and the other premiers argued that the British North America Act gave taxation powers to the provinces, not to Ottawa.

In 1947, Ontario and Quebec opted out of the so-called "tax rental" scheme, as was their constitutional right, and set up their own autonomous tax systems. Having the two levels of government assess and levy taxes proved inefficient, but beyond that, the danger arose a few years later that if Ottawa and the provinces could not agree on a peacetime tax regime, federal government spending that supported social reforms and the Korean war effort would be jeopardized. Moreover, if the federal government lacked the revenues to assist the less prosperous regions of the country, then the possibility existed that they, too, would opt out of the federal system of grants and payments and set about collecting their own revenues. Quebec, and to a lesser degree Ontario, wanted to turn back the clock to the 1930s when the provinces collected as much in taxes as Ottawa, thereby starving St. Laurent's government of the revenues it needed to fuel its "centralizing" domestic agenda.

After a prolonged series of battles with Quebec and Ontario, the federal government finally won agreement in 1957 for a revenue-sharing formula with the provinces. The old tax-rental scheme would be abandoned in favour of a program of "equalization." Provinces could collect a portion of the federal tax on individuals and corporations directly. Poorer provinces would be provided with grants that topped up their revenues based on a calculation that took into account the tax revenues of the two richest jurisdictions, Ontario and British Columbia. With equalization, the principle that Canadians in every province were entitled to similar services and standards of living became entrenched. As Walter Harris, a St. Laurent finance minister, observed some years later: "Every Canadian today believes that we should assist the provinces to provide a reasonable Canadian level of public service in all parts of Canada; nationhood would be meaningless if it were not so." Equalization, combined with federal social legislation, helped foster a loyalty to Canada the nation, even in those parts of the country, such as Quebec, that were traditionally wary of national programs and policies.

It is worth noting just how different the current fiscal relationship of the federal government to the provinces is from the original equalization system established in 1957. In the St. Laurent era, strict riders were put on how the provinces could spend federal funds for everything from roads to health care to post-secondary education. This would be anathema if not a political impossibility today when equalization payments, with few exceptions, are handed over to the provinces to spend as they see fit. So, too, would be the insistence of any federal government that the provinces automatically share in half the cost of nationally mandated programs, or go without. Built-in escalator clauses that increased equalization payments faster than the rate of inflation and provisions that gave the provinces ever more control over national programs in areas of shared jurisdiction have eroded the federal government's spending power and the corresponding ability of Ottawa to initiate large national projects.

The second and third pillars of the modern Canada that St. Laurent and his cabinet envisioned were culture and infrastructure.

In some circles, the anemic condition of Canadian culture— primarily in the arts, but also at the country's universities—was perceived as a sign of backwardness. Many, such as Lester Pearson, believed that if Canada was destined to play a larger role in world affairs, it should have the cultural hallmarks and institutions commensurate with its new-found international status.

In 1949, St. Laurent established the Royal Commission on National Development in the Arts, Letters and Sciences. It was chaired by former diplomat Vincent Massey (whose surname became the commission's more familiar moniker), and its recommendations shaped government policy in the arts, education and the media for an entire generation. New investments were made in the Canadian Broadcasting Corporation, especially in the new medium of television, and the mandate and resources of the National Film Board were expanded. Both agencies were seen as vehicles for Canadian identity in an era when American popular culture—its radio and television shows, films and magazines— were starting to claim large audiences in Canada. For the first time, significant federal funding was also provided to the country's universities, despite provincial protests against Ottawa's intrusions into yet another area of their "exclusive" jurisdiction.

Just as important to the country's maturing sense of itself was the creation of the arm's-length Canada Council for the Arts in 1957, with initial funding provided by a $100 million endowment derived from the death duties of two multi-millionaires, an investment equivalent to almost $1 billion today. The Council's brief went beyond the subsidization of "ballet dancing," as St. Laurent initially feared. It supported the study and production of works in the arts, the humanities and the social sciences, including those of such writers and academics as Marshall McLuhan and Harold Innis, scholars who were pursuing uniquely Canadian lines of inquiry into the country's history, politics and postwar society. The

Council also helped ensure the long-term viability of a raft of new Canadian performing arts organizations, such as the Stratford Festival, Le Théâtre du Nouveau Monde and, yes, the National Ballet of Canada. In tangible ways, the cultural policies of the St. Laurent government gave substance to the country's nascent, but palpable, nationalist mood.

In their size and complexity, the major infrastructure projects of these years shared the same spirit that had inspired the surge in public works initiated by the Reformers in the 1850s. Here the federal government took a far-sighted approach to creating new drivers for economic growth which sought to bind the country together through commerce and travel. C.D. Howe, the hard-driving "minister of everything" in St. Laurent's cabinet, announced the construction of the Trans-Canada Highway—a coast-to-coast highway built to a common, national standard— in the first year of the government's mandate. Ottawa would pay half of all construction costs, estimated initially at $150 million, and reimburse the provinces for any construction expenses along the agreed-upon route going back to 1928. One by one the provinces put aside their jurisdictional scruples, took the subsidy and allowed the federal government to get on with the job. Although the highway was not completed until 1965 and ended up costing close to a billion dollars, the project caught Canadians' imagination and put us on the road and into traffic jams and roadside diners for the balance of the century.

During this period, the federal government also made the major long-term investments that opened the St. Lawrence Seaway to large-scale shipping, developed an atomic energy industry and the first CANDU reactors, built new hydroelectric plants in Ontario and Quebec and contributed to the construction of the Distant Early Warning Line across the Arctic. Part of C.D. Howe's rationale for pouring hundreds of millions of dollars into these megaprojects was to create jobs and keep the economy humming. Equally importantly, though, they satisfied Canadians' ambitions for accomplishments on a grand scale.

The final task that St. Laurent and his colleagues set for themselves was to ground the country's civic culture, at home and abroad, on solidly North American foundations. This process unfolded in three acts. First, Canada's judicial arrangements with Britain were recast. In 1949, the Supreme Court of Canada, not the Judicial Committee of the Privy Council in Britain, became the court of final appeal for Canadians. Next, the British North America Act was amended to allow Canada's Parliament to change the Constitution in those areas that were the exclusive jurisdiction of the federal government. No longer would British Members of Parliament and Lords have the final word on Canada's constitutional evolution at the federal level. As a further symbol of autonomy from Britain, St. Laurent decided that Canada's next Governor General should be a Canadian, and in 1952 Ontario-born Vincent Massey was invested at Rideau Hall.

In 1947, Canadians were defined for the first time as citizens of Canada, not British subjects. The new Citizenship Act, championed by Paul Martin Sr., designated Canadian citizenship by birth and established the rules by which newcomers could acquire citizenship. In Martin's words, the "decision to clarify and regularize the status of Canadian citizenship constituted a major feat. Our membership in the family of nations had been recognized; we had won our certificate of nationhood...." Passage of the act was auspicious: throughout the 1950s, immigration from Europe held steady at over 100,000 people annually—a per capita rate of immigration equivalent to today's—and soared to close to 300,000 in 1956 when Hungarian refugees fleeing the Soviet invasion arrived in Canada.

The intent behind these policies concerning identity was not to sever the British connection. As political debates over the 1956 Suez Crisis would reveal, English Canadians could, at times, be fiercely loyal to their British heritage and quick to call their government to account for any perceived abandonment of the motherland. Rather, the goal was to reflect in laws, institutions and symbols, Canada's independent stature and its increasing self-confidence.

While Canadianizing symbols and political conventions at home, St. Laurent brought a North American focus to Canada's foreign policy and national defence policies. International events in the 1950s presented Canadians with a host of threats and challenges, most notably the deepening Cold War between the Soviet Union and the United States. Canada's dilemma was to find a way to be relevant internationally without simply exchanging its previous master, Britain, for a new overlord and protector, America. Typical of the period, Lester Pearson and a troika of brilliant diplomats—Escott Reid, Norman Robertson and Hume Wrong— decided to seize the initiative for Canada by proposing a new transatlantic military and economic alliance that would unite the democracies of western Europe and North America. Norman Robertson commented at the time, "The link across the North Atlantic seems to me such a proverbial solution for so many of our problems that I feel we should go to great lengths and even incur considerable risks in order to ensure our proper place in this new partnership."

The U.S. Congress was initially wary of the Canadian plan curtailing its military options in what was an explicitly multilateral defensive scheme, and it resisted Canada's insistence that the alliance also seek to create closer economic and political ties between member states. But after months of negotiations, Canada's all-out diplomatic push and the emergence of a parallel military pact linking Eastern Bloc nations under Soviet leadership persuaded the Americans to sign on to the North Atlantic Treaty Organization in 1949.

NATO provided Canada with the means to meld its historic relationship with Britain and its deepening strategic importance to America, thereby carving out for itself a realm of independent action and real international prominence. In effect, the country's historic ties to Britain and Europe remained intact, but during a Cold War in which American power became paramount to Canada's security and influence, these linkages were neither exclusive nor automatic.

The extent to which Canada succeeded in reinventing itself as a North American power was manifest in the two other international flashpoints of the 1950s: the Korean War and the Suez Crisis. Both demonstrated that the government of Canada was prepared to assume onerous obligations and to endure domestic dissent so that the country might assert itself on the world stage.

In the case of the Korean War, the country had to carry the financial burden of modernizing and quadrupling the size of Canada's postwar military to 120,000 men and women. The cost was staggering and forced trade-offs on domestic priorities, particularly regarding spending on social programs that voters believed were their due. The almost inconceivable sum of $5 billion was budgeted in 1951 for the Korean War and the country's Cold War commitments. Defence expenditures rose to an astounding 7 percent of the country's entire GDP in 1952, the last year of the Korean conflict.

Public opinion in Quebec was against the war on the grounds that it represented another English Canadian entanglement, with all the additional dangers inherent to the new atomic age. Yet, in the face of blatant Communist aggression and the need to support Canada's traditional allies, St. Laurent felt compelled to risk the ire of his fellow French Canadians and make a major commitment to the United Nations force. In the end, Canada sent some 26,000 armed forces personnel along with transport aircraft and ships. Three-plus years, 1,500 wounded and 516 dead later, Canada's Korean War was over.

In the case of the Suez Crisis, far less Canadian blood and treasure was wagered, but the prize was no less significant. When Britain and France, with Israel's assistance, moved against Egypt in retaliation against that country's nationalization of the vital Suez Canal in 1956, NATO pact relations were severely tested. The Americans had been blindsided by the invasion in the last days of a presidential election and, along with Canada, opposed Britain and France's unilateral action. They believed it would set the developing world against the West and provide the Soviets with a propaganda coup at the very moment they were invading Hungary. Through sheer force of will, Lester Pearson was able to bring the British and French, the Americans and the balance of the United Nations General Assembly around to supporting the deployment of the first-ever large international peacekeeping force, a body that included Canadian troops. The fighting was halted, and a Canadian and international icon was born: the blue-helmeted peacekeeper.

Pearson won the Nobel Peace Prize for his efforts but, just as importantly, Canada's postwar foreign policy was validated. "The early breakdown between the Big Powers and the United Nations made the position of the Middle Powers such as Canada important," Pearson said later. "They stood between the increasing number of small states that had little power and the great states which had too much." Indeed, in those harrowing days in 1956, Canada and Lester Pearson could rightly claim to be the pivot point of the entire Anglo-American relationship.

LESSONS LEARNED

Considered collectively, the policies and institutions put into place by the St. Laurent government established the essential shape of modern Canada. In a nine-year period, the country entrenched the concept of universality in the design and delivery of social programs, a keystone of the welfare state that was expanded over subsequent decades. So, too, with a host of other national projects and symbols that we commonly associate with Canada's coming of age, from Canadian-born Governors General to the Trans-Canada Highway. On the world stage, Canada demonstrated its hard-won autonomy from Britain by paying its own way—and then some—when it came to national defence, even if that meant delaying spending on social programs in order to do our share of the heavy lifting in the Korean War, in NATO and at the United Nations.

The reasons for this record of sustained accomplishment went beyond Canada's strong economy of the 1950s or the opportunity to play middle power to the Cold War's superpowers. It is conceivable that the federal government might have turned its tax surpluses over to the provinces in perpetuity in 1948, a move that would have been applauded in Quebec and Ontario. Or it could have diminished its revenues with short-term tax cuts or popular but unsustainable social programs. It could have left the defence of Canada and the free world to the United States. Instead, in less than a decade, the federal government moved boldly to establish the national and international institutions upon which much of Canadians' sense of common purpose would rest for the balance of the century.

The success of the St. Laurent government's nation building measures flowed from three factors. The first was the war and its impact on the attitudes of the country's leaders and its citizens concerning the role of the federal government and national institutions. Beyond relief at the defeat of Fascism, the war's end brought a determination to build a more humane society back home, as the war itself had educated a generation of leaders about the potential of central institutions and strong national government to accomplish remarkable things for the common good. There would be no going back to the decentralized Canada of the pre-war period, when both levels of government had equivalent revenues and the ability to initiate social policy was left to the provinces. Rather, the constitutional power and the political heft of the federal government were put in service of the wholesale reform of Canadian domestic policy. By the decade's end, individual Canadians' lives had been changed— and overwhelmingly for the better—by national government and national institutions.

The second factor that propelled St. Laurent's nation building agenda was Canada's increasingly important and independent role as a country that stood first among the middle powers. In the 1950s, we were an ambitious people who remembered the great things we had accomplished during the war and who expected our future to hold similar triumphs. Lester Pearson's Nobel Peace Prize was not only a singular honour in its own right, it was a symbol of what Canada could achieve in the larger theatre of world affairs. In effect, the effort to define who we were as a people took on a permanent international dimension during this period. The degree to which we could successfully assert a national identity distinct from that of Britain and especially the United States was seen as dependent on Canada's continuing contribution to world affairs, both diplomatically and militarily. The key role Canada played in the creation of NATO, during the Korean War and at the United Nations as well as its record levels of defence spending, were as much an expression of our national identity as they were efforts to make the country secure and give it a say in the direction of world affairs.

Finally, there was a new mood in the country itself, one that supported an activist federal government and the creation of national institutions to promote the public good. Perhaps for the first time since Confederation, Canadians had a renewed sense of themselves as neither subjects of the British Empire nor paler and poorer cousins of the Americans, but as a nation with its own unique values and interests. In the 1950s, Canadians had, in effect, recaptured the spirit of Louis LaFontaine and Robert Baldwin. We had returned to the task of making real, through national institutions, an identity that was egalitarian in character, economically ambitious and collectively self-confident. It was a moment when Canadians once again knew who they were.

SO WHAT HAPPENED?

The belief in national government and national institutions as the most effective means to improve Canadians' lives did, however, not endure. Nor did the idea that Canada's international stature required substantial outlays on national defence. The same was true of the conviction that major investments in the country's infrastructure, competitive taxes rates and a healthy dose of individual self-reliance should take precedence over unsustainable spending on cradle-to-grave social programs. So what happened? Why did our faith in the efficacy of national government and federal institutions, our concept of the country's role in the world and our appetite for nation building alter so drastically in the last decades of the twentieth century?

Historians have typically focussed on the major social changes that occurred in the sixties, seventies and eighties to explain the forces that transformed the country's view of its long-term goals and sense of itself. As mentioned earlier, this makes sense; it is impossible to disassociate, say, the Quiet Revolution and two Quebec referendums on separation from our perceptions of federalism today. Similarly, the advent of the modern welfare state with its vast array of programs—childcare, job training, regional development, old-age pensions, universal medicare, mothers' allowances and more—changed forever our expectations of the role and function of government in our day-to-day lives. So, too, did the coming-of-age of the baby-boom generation. New social mores, the Vietnam War and a generation's distrust of institutionalized authority all combined to refashion the country's foreign policy and domestic priorities. High immigration from increasingly non-European places also changed the country's international interests and refocussed domestic attention on social programs and official multiculturalism. Add to this mix two severe recessions, growing anxiety about America's economic dominance and the changes wrought by globalization, and it is not surprising that Canada met the new century with reduced expectations both for nation building at home and for direct influence abroad.

These trends, with the possible exception of high immigration, were predictable. They affected most advanced democracies, and on balance Canadians adjusted well. What has long interested me, however, is how the country's leaders, in the decades following Louis St. Laurent's back-to-back majority governments, continued to reimagine the Canadian identity. In the visions of nationhood that emerged in the 1960s and 1970s we find a series of new assumptions about the goals of Canadian society that were quite different from those of St. Laurent and his generation.

One major change was the re-emergence of anti-Americanism as a powerful cultural force. As we have seen, the United Empire Loyalists were first and foremost anti-Americans, and part of their legacy was to hardwire into Canada's political culture an innate distrust of American society. Throughout the nineteenth century and the first half of the twentieth, our politics were tinged with an anti-American worldview that periodically exploded into divisive national debates, usually revolving around our economic relationship with America. Part of what made St. Laurent's governments unique were their self-assured and generally non-agonistic ways of dealing with the U.S. This attitude was born of war and the confidence it had given Canadians, accompanied by a generally buoyant feeling about the country's prospects. It was also made necessary by the common security challenges to both nations as the Cold War got underway. We had a surer vision of the country's future as an honest broker between American and European interests and a focussed national agenda of modest but effective social reform and infrastructure investments. On balance, Canada's foreign interests and domestic priorities, not a fear of American cultural, economic or military power, drove policy-making at the national and international levels.

But old suspicions of the southern neighbour die hard, as do the political rewards that anti-Americanism can bestow on a savvy national leader or party. Concerns about growing U.S. ownership of Canadian businesses—one of the issues Diefenbaker used to defeat St. Laurent at the polls and end twenty-two years of Liberal rule—re-emerged in the 1960s and 1970s as a salient feature of the national political debate. Various attempts were made to limit American investment, culminating in the creation of the Foreign Investment Review Agency in 1973, along with quixotic efforts to diversify Canada's export markets. Also in the 1970s, the federal government got into the business of buying control in major Canadian enterprises that were thought to be vulnerable to U.S. takeover. From the creation of Petro-Canada to the disastrous National Energy Program to the subsidization of entire industries, billions of dollars in government funding were vaporized in the act of saving Canada from the supposed perils of an economic "Americanization" that national leaders of all stripes shamelessly decried for political advantage.

More serious than the raft of government policies and programs aimed at reducing the economic impact of the United States on Canada was the effect of anti-Americanism on our conversations about ourselves. The tendency from the late 1960s onwards to define what it meant to be Canadian not on its own terms or in the context of our own history, but as the opposite of, or radically different from being American, eroded the self-confidence that had taken hold of the country during the St. Laurent and Pearson eras.

In terms of domestic policy, this thrust began in earnest in the late 1960s when federal social programs and universal health care were increasingly justified not on ethical grounds—as their precursors had largely been by St. Laurent and Paul Martin Sr.—but because they served to differentiate Canada from the United States. Put another way, the willingness of our governments to enact policies that aligned Canadian and American economic interests or domestic approaches decreased as fears of the American threat to our cultural and economic independence increased in the public's imagination. The persistence of this mindset placed entire government institutions and programs beyond the realm of rational analysis and discussion. A case in point is our health care system: any meaningful public debate over how to reform health care delivery has been stifled by a generation of national leaders prophesying that any substantial overhaul risks "Americanizing" the Canadian model.

The same inertia confused and postponed the difficult, but necessary, conversations Canadians should have had about the sustainability of the country's ever expanding social programs or about whether or not its national interests were being advanced by its foreign and defence policies. The irony is that our obsession with insulating Canadian policy debates from the influence of "American" ideas or interests meant that Canadians became even more affected by what the United States did or did not do.

The re-emergence of anti-Americanism diverted or excused Canada's leaders, along with many of its national institutions, from continuing the efforts of St. Laurent's generation to define what Canada was, and what it might become, on its own terms. Historian Jack Granatstein sums up the long-term effect of our anti-Americanism best: "With all its hatred, bias, and deliberately contrived fear-mongering, anti-Americanism became the Canadian way of being different."

Another significant misstep by subsequent federal governments was the abandonment of the defence and foreign affairs policies that had given Canada its international raison d'être at mid-century. St. Laurent and Pearson understood a basic truth: modern Canada's sense of itself as an independent and confident nation rested, in no small part, on its international accomplishments and capabilities. They correctly saw Canada as a key member of the "Anglosphere," a nation tied by history to Europe, but with values and security needs closely aligned to those of the United States. Canadians' support for multilateral institutions such as the United Nations and their interest in aiding the developing world were sincere, but Canada's leaders knew that the country's foreign interests were best advanced by significant investments in national defence and a foreign policy attuned to great-power politics. It was our military strength and close relationships with the United States and Britain, not our status as a moral superpower, that gave Canada a seat at the table of the world's major political and economic bodies.

The foreign policy lessons of the St. Laurent years were all but lost on the generation of Canadians who came of age politically in the shadow of the Vietnam War. The new mantra was that Americans were the warmongers, and Canadians the peacemakers. An already anemic military budget was further reduced by successive governments and remains, at this writing, at less than 2 percent of GDP. The country's foreign policy consciously and consistently deviated from that of its traditional allies, Britain and the United States, as much for domestic political consumption as for the advancement of any real national interest or priority. For Canadian policy-makers, multilateralism, not bilateralism, became the reigning ideology. The country joined countless international associations and issue-based groups that further diffused Canada's influence where it mattered most, that being in the capitals of Europe and in Washington. At the low point of our relations with the U.S., we cheered on Trudeau and others who courted Cuba's Castro and dallied with the leaders of the non-aligned states, the majority of whom were brutal dictators.

The consequences of this effort to uncouple Canadian foreign policy from bilateral and military relationships with our allies were predictable. Canada's international influence waned, and with it public support for military spending and for the financial outlays required by a vigorous foreign policy and effective development assistance programs. Arguably, the prestige of the federal government in Canadians' eyes also fell as its leadership in this one area of exclusive constitutional jurisdiction evaporated. By the turn of the century, Canada was a country that had withdrawn into itself, retreating from the centre stage of the global commons in a manner that surely must have set Louis St. Laurent and Lester B. Pearson spinning in their graves.

In addition to these downshifts in international standing and economic and cultural self-confidence vis-à-vis the United States, I would single out one more major transformation in our interpretation of the nature and purpose of Canada in the post–St. Laurent era. Starting in the 1960s and accelerating through the 1970s and 1980s, Canadians began to self-consciously shed their awareness of the country's nineteenth-century history. After a particularly bitter parliamentary and public debate, the Red Ensign was replaced by the Maple Leaf Flag. The Dominion government became the federal government, and later, Dominion Day was replaced by Canada Day. The word "Royal" in the names of Crown agencies was replaced by "Canada." The bicultural foundation of Canadian nationhood was augmented with a multicultural pillar supporting the idea that the country was made up of various minority groups that defined themselves as unique and wished to remain so. These changes, along with countless others, were all part and parcel of a systematic and sustained overhaul of the country's institutions, symbols and civic traditions.

On one level, the politics that inspired this overhaul could be seen a continuation of the program of Canadianization that had been embraced by St. Laurent and his contemporaries. In the immediate postwar period, Canada had sensibly asserted its autonomy from Britain in all the ways described earlier. But the debate at the time was never one of how Canada could set about erasing its colonial heritage in name or fact. In our political traditions and civic culture, the country was thoroughly British and a proud and active member of the Commonwealth of Nations. These symbols and linkages were seen by the leaders of the day as a good thing in terms of differentiating Canada from the U.S. and maintaining a civic patrimony that had served the country admirably for more than a century.

The intent and the extent of subsequent governments' deracination of the country's colonial symbols and traditions were qualitatively different from the reforms introduced during the St. Laurent years. The rebranding of our national symbols was driven not simply by a desire to assert the country's cultural and political independence from Britain; its goal was to sever the identity of modern Canada from much of its historical moorings, a past that was perceived to be made up mostly of wars, colonialism and interracial and inter-regional conflicts. By blotting out our nineteenth-century origins, the country could supposedly avoid further provoking Quebec nationalists—a major preoccupation at the time. The desire to liberate Canada from the cultural and political encumbrances of its colonial past was also fuelled by the view that the new ethnic groups immigrating to Canada would feel unconnected to this history. Allegedly, the country would do a better job of settling newcomers if the institutions of the Canadian state adopted multiculturalism and promoted the notion that Canada was made up of many equivalent identities rather than a single overarching civic creed.

Thankfully, there has been some awareness recently of the costs of the country's ahistorical turn in the latter half of the twentieth century. Jettisoning the symbols and institutions associated with our nineteenth-century civic traditions has arguably undercut English Canada's attempt to maintain a cultural identity separate from the United States. As George Grant and others have observed, an English-Canadian political culture weakened by the denial of its own unique history could be seen as having contributed to, rather than eased, French Canadians' doubts that the rest of Canada was still committed to building a society along non-American and non-assimilative lines.

Obscuring Canada's traditional symbols and civic traditions also made it more difficult for a culturally diverse country to forge those essential bonds of citizenship and community that all nations depend upon. Newcomers to Canada, if they were exposed to Canadian history at all, were fed a watered-down version that focussed on the country's recent past—primarily post-Second-World-War history—and the rights and privileges of citizenship.

The historical narrative presented in schools and in popular culture today remains largely bereft of the civic lessons that past generations derived from the stories associated with the country's journey from colony to nation-state: its military triumphs, its struggle for democracy and its bicultural foundations.

Just as problematic is the fact that many of the symbols and institutions that supplanted the civic culture derived from the struggle for responsible government and Confederation sparked new controversies and divisions. For instance, while the Charter of Rights and Freedoms is a source of pride for many Canadians and a defining symbol of modern Canada, it has undeniably made our civic culture more American in its assertion of the primacy of the rights of individuals and groups over community norms. Certainly, the Charter has contributed to the decline of the influence and power of Parliament and the democratic process, both historically prominent aspects of Canadians' and especially Quebecers' efforts to articulate a common identity and shared social aims. Nowhere is this dynamic more evident than within the Supreme Court itself. In the era of the Charter, Canada's highest court has become the first, and increasingly the last, forum for not just the discussion but the mediation and working-through of the major social, political and economic issues facing the country.

In the same vein, the onus we placed on our health care system, on peacekeeping and on an expanding roster of social programs as the symbols of modernity and Canada's progress was fine in principle, but what happens to our sense of national identity and belonging when these institutions are overtaken by events or circumstances on the ground? It is far from clear that Canadians today have the same sense of allegiance to, or confidence in, the large-scale social programs and institutions that were created in the 1960s and 1970s. Whether it is our health care system, creaking under the growing financial burden of an aging population, or the steady leaching of federal power and prestige to the provinces or the fact that we are fighting a war, not leading a peacekeeping mission, in Afghanistan, many of our previously comfortable and well-worn notions of what defined Canada in the time of Pearson and Trudeau have been undermined or are being tested like never before.

Indeed, I would argue that the absence of the traditions that evoke the civic legacy of past generations haunts us like a lost limb. We know from certain periods in our history that Canada is a nation whose greatness is founded on more than individual liberty alone. We know that the sum of who we are is greater than the programs and institutions of the government of the day. But thanks to an intentionally induced amnesia surrounding the democratic origins and symbols of our civic culture, the path back to a shared understanding of the country's nature and purpose—a path that relies on more than our besieged national institutions or a social contract based, U.S.–style, on individual and group rights—is anything but obvious.

7 | OUR THIRD IMAGINING

THOSE who would have us believe that Canada has always been a contingent association of different regions, linguistic groups and ethnic communities ignore or have forgotten the story of our evolution as a civic nation. History shows that ours is a political community built on shared democratic values and institutions rather than on ethnicity, region or language.

Our coming of age began in the aftermath of the American Revolution when the colonies of British North America were convulsed by the bitter politics of loyalty. The issues that consumed our forebears centred on the shifting and fragile allegiances of a massive influx of immigrants, first from the United States and then from Britain. Would these rough-and-ready settlers remain obedient to the executive fiat of the Governors General and the colonial elites? Or would America's ideals of revolution and individual freedom fire their imaginations? Or, worst of all, would the imported hatreds of distant homelands ignite existing linguistic and religious divisions and plunge the Canadian colonies into intractable sectarian strife?

Thanks to the tenacity and courage of a small group of French and English Reformers, each of these alternative futures was ultimately rejected. They were rejected because the Reformers asked an entirely different question, one that galvanized the colonies of British North America: what would it mean to be loyal to Canada?

For Louis LaFontaine, Robert Baldwin, Joseph Howe and their immediate successors, loyalty to Canada meant a lifelong commitment to the idea of a free and equal citizenry engaged in a great democratic experiment. It meant creating political institutions, chief among them responsible government, that brought the colonies' disparate factions together in the common project of political reform, not revolution. It meant establishing non-sectarian institutions of higher learning and free public education. It meant bringing government closer to the people by allowing for the election of local councils and empowering towns and cities to collect their own taxes and fund public works. It meant instituting sweeping land and legal reforms and abolishing preferential treatment for the established church and the Tory elite. And it meant using the nascent power of the state to initiate important national projects—canals, roads and railways—that would spur economic development and commerce.

All of these policies were intended to advance a single goal: the establishment of a new nation, Canada, as an egalitarian, democratic, economically ambitious and less sectarian society—a wholly Canadian vision that was consciously distinct from Britain's and America's. The period that began with the achievement of responsible government in 1848 and culminated with Confederation in 1867 established the civic trajectory of our society: the conviction that we are equal participants in an evolving democratic project that seeks to reconcile our individual differences within common institutions and civic values.

Yes, Canada has stumbled, and repeatedly, from the path our founders set out on more than 160 years ago. Systemic racism against the Aboriginal population, the hanging of Louis Riel, the head tax on Chinese immigrants, the mindless imperialism that sucked us into the grist mills of the Boer War and the Great War, the conscription crises of both world wars and the two Quebec referendums and the near breakup of the country are all boldfaced items on a list of collective sins of omission and commission.

Yet despite these setbacks, the country remained true for the next hundred years to the original objectives that Canadians had embraced at the midpoint of the nineteenth century. The governments of Louis St. Laurent in particular reinforced and advanced those ideals after the Second World War, a period when the country's sense of itself was once again in flux. Like the mid-1800s, the 1950s represented a crucial juncture, a time when we could have recast the country's identity in ways that would not have been true to our history but would have mimicked the animating concepts of British or American society. Instead, we reconnected, through conscious effort, with the grand narrative that had launched our nation a century before.

The parallels between the two periods are striking. Megaprojects such as the Trans-Canada Highway and the St. Lawrence Seaway were the modern-day equivalents of the canals, roads and railways constructed by LaFontaine, Howe and Baldwin to bind the colonies together in commerce and industry. Like the Reformers of the 1840s, St. Laurent and his generation sought to give life and shape to what our forebears called "a provincial feeling" by investing massively in public education and by treating immigration as an economic opportunity, not a cultural threat. Both generations, though a century apart, understood and respected the desire to Canadianize the country's British political conventions, institutions and symbols without abandoning British parliamentary traditions or historically rooted civic values.

The particular genius of St. Laurent and his governments was to refashion for their own times the democratic project instigated by LaFontaine, Howe and Baldwin. They used the levers of national government to create nationwide programs such as universal health insurance, old-age pensions and equalization, measures that bolstered the conviction that we owed our ultimate loyalty to each other as equal participants in a national enterprise, irrespective of region or social class. Just as importantly, St. Laurent's governments understood that asserting Canada's distinctness from Britain and the United States went beyond the realms of domestic policy. Whether it was our leading role in the creation of NATO, our significant contribution to the Korean War or our timely breakthroughs in diplomacy, the imperative first articulated by the Reformers to seek out an alternative "Canadian way" became an outward-looking project with international ramifications.

WHO WE ARE

This history bears repeating. I believe that the first step in reclaiming the shared values and social solidarity essential to our future well-being is to remember that Canada was founded and has evolved as a nation of citizens, not a collection of communities. We are a people who long operated according to a series of hard-won principles and beliefs about the purpose of our society.

First, we are suspicious of anything that hints of sectarianism. Hard-wired into our collective memory is an awareness of the harm nineteenth-century sectarian variants caused to the country, of the ways in which individual liberty was stifled by forces that defined our forebears first and foremost as members of a group or faction. We know all too well how religious and ethnic divisions, if left unchecked, compound themselves and become intractable obstacles to economic and social progress. This legacy has taught us that if we are to function as free and autonomous citizens, our highest loyalty must be to the country's unique political conventions, to the institutions and practices of our democracy that allow us to broker competing interests and personal beliefs and act in common enterprise.

Second, we are strong believers in public institutions, generally the most efficacious expressions of both deeply held values and national aspirations. For the better part of our history, we have looked beyond the words of the Canadian Constitution to those institutions that act as instruments of the country's core beliefs. Institutions such as responsible government, biculturalism and public education are more than just expressions of our values at a particular moment in time. They represent a distillation of the choices we have made, over decades and even centuries, about the ways in which the country should operate and the principles to which it is dedicated.

Third, we subscribe to the idea of Canadian exceptionalism. Whether it be one generation's pride in being the first British colony to achieve responsible government or another generation's genius in creating modern-day peacekeeping, we seek out the "Canadian way" that will distinguish us from our peers. Furthermore, we have long believed that Canada's destiny is unique and that we have a responsibility to discover and foster the sources of our exceptionalism. And this we have done: time and again, we have committed ourselves to nation-changing policies—the most recent being world leadership in immigration—that ensure that the country's future will be neither European nor American, but something all its own.

Fourth, we are a people who, historically, relished ambitious national projects; the sheer size of Canada challenged us to gird the country with railways, highways and canals. At an elemental level, the country's early nation builders wanted to see their prowess reflected in the physical mastery of Canada's continental landmass. As we matured as a country, our impulse for national building took on an added dimension, giving substance to the values and beliefs that united us. Here the postwar generation turned to the Canadian state and used its powers to build not only physical infrastructure, but twentieth-century social and economic programs that reflected our mutual goals and aspirations just as surely as the nineteenth century's railways, waterways and roads.

Fifth, we are an egalitarian people. We do not think that the accident of birth should determine the course of an individual's life or that the wealthy and privileged few should unduly influence the direction of our society. The breadth of the voting franchise at the country's democratic beginnings and the non-denominational religious impulses of many of Canada's early settlers had a long-term levelling effect on our civic and political culture. So, too, did the Reformers' sweeping political innovations that empowered local communities and introduced meritocracy into the administration of government and the judiciary. Canadians' commitment to creating a more equal society was entrenched by St. Laurent's affirmation of the concept of universality in national programs.

I would add to this list of defining elements one last feature: we are an ambitious people. Contrary to the view that Canadians are a cautious bunch, one has only to read about our struggle for democracy or our efforts to claim a voice for Canada in world affairs to know that we are a nation that has consistently taken bold, occasionally even reckless, steps to assert ourselves. As we know, such undertakings as the construction of the Canadian Pacific Railway, the defence of freedom in the Second World War and Cold War and the ongoing project of welcoming millions of immigrants from the world over have stretched us in unpredictable, but inspiring, ways.

If we take to heart these six core beliefs about what it means to be Canadian, then a different perspective on our current predicaments and their potential solutions opens up. We cannot deal with the various challenges facing our country today and in the future in isolation. Instead, we must find a rallying cause to which we can summon the country's latent civic energy. Just as responsible government called to the Reformers in the 1840s and national programs and the power of the federal government motivated St. Laurent and his contemporaries in the 1950s, so must we identify an inspiring and animating objective for our own times.

This single idea needs to speak to the reality of Canada today, not some idealized past or hypothetical future. And it must evoke the constellation of first principles that have given our society its momentum over the last century and a half: our sense of loyalty to each other, our egalitarian impulses, our belief in the power of public institutions, Canadian exceptionalism, nation building and, last but not least, raw national ambition and competitiveness vis-à-vis our peer nations. Fortunately, there is one such vehicle: the concept of Canadian citizenship.

Citizenship—by which I mean the laws, institutions and symbols that define our individual membership in the Canadian nation—has the potential to raise our sights again. In fact, a revitalized citizenship may be the best and last hope for Canadians ready to rid themselves of their "postnational" ennui and reconnect with the enduring values and principles upon which Canada's greatness rests.

CIVIS CANADENSIS SUM

The notion of citizenship may seem a dubious rallying point for a country as diverse and decentralized as Canada. As we have seen, Canadian citizenship carries with it few substantive obligations or duties. In the words of Desmond Morton, "By the standards of most European nations, the citizenship that Ottawa created in 1946 and amended in 1976 is easy and undemanding. In peace and even in war, a strong historical prejudice protects Canadians from compulsory military service…For those who chose to be naturalized, the residence requirement is conveniently brief…The requirement of 'adequate' knowledge of Canada has to be modest lest it embarrass the native-born."

The Charter of Rights and Freedoms makes few distinctions between the rights afforded citizens and those given non-citizens within Canada. The difference amounts to the right to vote in elections, to seek election to the House of Commons or a provincial legislature, to move freely in and out of Canada and, where applicable, to send one's children to minority language schools. All the other rights citizens enjoy are granted to non-citizens who are "physically present in Canada." If a growing number of big-city mayors get their way, non-citizens may soon be able to vote in municipal elections. On the surface, our common citizenship seems unlikely to spark Canadians' interest in nation building or reawaken their sense of shared purpose.

I would suggest, however, that this is the case only if one is looking at Canada's twenty-first-century challenges through twentieth-century eyes. Take, for instance, my favourite troika of forces most likely to shape Canada's future: climate change, an aging population and continuing high levels of immigration. All share one common feature: they will severely strain the country's already weakened bonds of social solidarity. Together they will exert tremendous pressures on the country's political institutions and call into question long-standing assumptions about how our federation works. And, as political scientist Thomas Homer-Dixon reminds us, although "everything looks relatively calm on the surface, it doesn't mean everything is fine underneath…shifts in a society's complexity and interconnectedness, in the quality of the resources it depends on and in its relations with its natural environment can make a society progressively more vulnerable to sudden, sharp and enormously disruptive bursts of change."

Given the scale and inevitability of these phenomena, it is reasonable to expect that the bonds of community and mutual responsibility that exist today will be stressed to an extent we have not experienced in living memory. This is why I believe that beyond our current preoccupations with health care funding, our economic fundamentals and the war in Afghanistan, there exists a greater, overarching issue. How do we restore—and quickly— the sense of social solidarity required to survive an era of rapid change? How do we replenish the reserves of social capital and civic literacy that we know from past experience are essential to the smooth functioning of a society as complex as Canada's?

It is here that citizenship, the neglected and often slighted poor cousin of national symbols, could play an important, if not essential, role. Equipped with meaningful obligations as well as strong incentives for civic-minded behaviour, our shared citizenship could strengthen and deepen our social networks and encourage the kind of participation in political groups, voluntary organizations and service clubs that builds trust between individuals and creates the impetus to pursue common aims. Even more significantly for pluralistic societies such as Canada's, a robust vision of the responsibilities of citizenship, applied equally to both newcomers and longer-settled Canadians, could go far in cultivating the social capital that bridges the divides of ethnicity, class and region.

Along with healthy reserves of social capital, high rates of civic literacy are essential to sustaining a society's overall levels of participation in formal politics. Obviously, we want a society that is politically active and informed; the nurturing of these traits is our best guarantee of preserving our collective way of life. Here, too, a reassertion of our shared citizenship that champions, in our schools and in the naturalization process for newcomers, the basic responsibility to know something about the country in which we each claim membership could be a powerful tool.

In sum, a reimagined and reinvigorated Canadian citizenship has the potential to provide the conceptual and institutional framework for programs and policies that will replenish our diminished stocks of cultural capital, civic literacy and social solidarity that will be necessary to weather the upheavals of the century ahead.

CITIZENSHIP AND NEWCOMERS

We need to begin by acknowledging that Canadian citizenship has never been worth more than it is today. The country's long-term economic fundamentals are strong when compared with those of other advanced nations. In a world afflicted with ever more failing and failed states, Canada's geographic advantages are clear, its social and political climate highly attractive. Canada has become one of the world's most desirable addresses. I would argue that the present comparative advantages of being Canadian, for both aspiring citizens and the Canadian-born, represent an unparalleled opportunity to engage the country in an overhaul of the institutions and laws of Canadian citizenship, one that could serve to promote social capital and civic literacy.

Putting Down Roots

Let's begin with aspiring citizens, those who are seeking to come to Canada. Given the considerable benefits Canada affords, it is reasonable to ask newcomers to assume greater responsibilities and forge deeper commitments to the country than has traditionally been expected of immigrants. Currently, the process of acquiring citizenship in Canada is among the least demanding of the family of the nations that actively encourage high rates of legal immigration. For example, once an individual has been granted permanent residence status, full citizenship can be acquired after three years, or 1,095 days, of residency in Canada within a four-year period. Our citizenship laws also allow applicants to leave the country for work, business or family reasons for up to six months each year they are completing their residency requirement. By comparison, the United States and Great Britain require five years of permanent residency with less latitude for leaves of absence; Germany requires eight years.

The length of an immigrant's residency period is important. It helps ensure the acquisition of language skills, a significant factor given that one in three immigrants Canada accepted in recent years declared no knowledge of French or English. Some basic language ability is essential to securing a job and therefore to helping raise income levels among newcomers. It is also a prerequisite for participation in the kinds of civic associations and community groups that promote cultural integration and foster social capital. A residency requirement of five years, with stricter rules as to how long and for what reasons permanent residents may leave the country, could deter so-called "citizens of convenience" who are interested in acquiring a Canadian passport but have little inclination to take up permanent residence or contribute to Canada, within Canada, on an ongoing basis.

A New Citizenship Exam

We should follow the leads of Australia, Britain and the United States and overhaul the twenty-year-old examination that immigrants are required to pass to become citizens. According to Dominion Institute research, newcomers take the current citizenship exam very seriously and as a result attain levels of basic civic literacy higher than those of native-born Canadians. Let's build on this dedication and encourage the good things that come with high civic literacy, such as voting and participation in formal politics, by designing a more comprehensive exam that covers a range of subjects related to Canada's history, political system and the responsibilities of citizenship. The current practice of asking newcomers to identify Canada's official languages from a list of choices that includes German and Italian is an insult to their intelligence and does nothing to promote a deeper appreciation of their adopted nation. Let's also do away with the practice of allowing citizenship judges to administer the exam orally, often with the applicant's lawyer acting as "translator."

And since the ability to speak French or English is so critical to an immigrant's economic success and overall social integration, let's make a moderate or high proficiency in reading, writing and speaking either official language a prerequisite for every person applying to come to Canada as a skilled worker or professional. For the majority of newcomers who come as dependents of the primary applicant, we need to redouble our efforts to ensure that these individuals attain basic language proficiency as quickly as possible. Specifically, the adult-aged dependents of primary applicants should receive in-depth language testing as part of the citizenship exam process. Based on the assessment they receive, they should have the opportunity to continue language training beyond the current three-year cut-off. Basic language proficiency is especially important for immigrant women. Having entered Canada as spouses of the primary applicant and therefore not pre-screened for language proficiency, women are significantly more likely than their male counterparts to lack a working knowledge of French or English. From a social-justice perspective, this is a situation that must be addressed so that every female newcomer, regardless of their country of origin or initial language ability, has the fluency to participate fully in the country's democratic institutions.

In addition to focussing on the language needs of women, the federal government should put special emphasis on second-language training for school-age children, particularly in Vancouver, Toronto and Montreal. Young people from non-French- or English-speaking countries need additional support to master French and/or English, and the federal government should find ways to work with the provinces to get funding for targeted language instruction into the classrooms to relieve overburdened ESL instructors.

Dual Citizens Pay

Canada's policies concerning dual citizenship need to be liberated from the spurious notion that the lack of civic obligations attached to Canadian citizenship is a strategic asset in a world of multiple identities and allegiances. As Canadians witnessed during the evacuation of 15,000 Canadian nationals from Lebanon in 2006 (of which an estimated 7,000 returned to Lebanon almost immediately), citizens who live permanently outside the country enjoy some remarkable privileges with few, if any, obligations.

In addition to the expectation that they will be rescued if caught up in violent conflicts abroad, Canada's 1.7 million or so non-resident citizens are eligible for resident tuition fees at Canadian colleges and universities (a benefit worth up to $50,000 that does not include the substantial government subsidies each institution receives to fund spaces for students) and free public health care after six months of residence in Canada, with the ability to pass all of these benefits on to their spouses and children.

Even without calculating the consequences for our overburdened cities and social services of a mass return of hundreds of thousands of non-residents because of an environmental crisis or a regional war, we know that these dual citizenship policies are costing the country tens of millions of dollars each year in consular services and subsidized tuition and health care, with little or no economic or civic benefit. Canada, like the United States, should tax non-residents on their worldwide earnings and charge a hefty fee for renewing their Canadian passports. Yes, there is a cost associated with collecting these taxes, and the taxes themselves would not represent a big financial windfall, but the principle is critical: permanent non-residents should not enjoy a free ride when the benefits of Canadian citizenship continue to appreciate.

The scant difference between the rights afforded citizens living in Canada and those given to Canadians living abroad also devalues the contributions of every immigrant who makes Canada his or her permanent home. In fact, our lax dual citizenship policy and residency requirements run contrary to our historical understanding of citizenship. The opening decades of the nineteenth century eventually saw the triumph of the belief that, regardless of what religion you practiced or whether you were born in America or Britain, you could acquire full membership in colonial society. Then, as it should be now, full citizenship and all the benefits it bestowed were something that was earned through physical settlement and by contributing over time to the economic and social betterment of the community.

Everyone's Responsibility

In a world where personal mobility is the norm, will a more demanding citizenship, along with real costs and responsibilities for dual citizenship, drive away the very skilled immigrants we need to shore up our workforce? Although this is a valid question, it reflects the mindset of an earlier era when we ourselves viewed Canadian citizenship as the consolation prize for not becoming an American. The reality is that despite our high levels of overall annual immigration, we welcomed a paltry 60,000 skilled and professional immigrants in 2008, or about one in four of the total number of individuals who settled in Canada that year. The balance was comprised of dependents (mainly spouses and children), refugees and family unification cases. When we think of the universe of skilled workers who might consider applying for Canadian citizenship—the slightly more than three billion people who make up the emerging economies of India, China, Indonesia and Brazil—it can be argued that the attractions of Canada will more than outweigh the increased responsibilities associated with the reforms outlined here. Indeed, if we acknowledge the extent to which the value of Canadian citizenship will increase in a period of climate disruption, resource scarcity and global instability, we can improve the immigration system in ways that genuinely benefit the country, increase our intake of skilled newcomers and deter citizens of convenience.

As was demonstrated by the story of the immigrant who had made up his mind to leave Canada and return to his home in India with his wife and children, the problem with our immigration and settlement systems lies not in attracting desirable immigrants; it is in keeping them. In my view, our failure to retain newcomers has as much to do with our society's low levels of social solidarity and civic engagement as it does with economic considerations.

There are a number of practical policies we can put into place to help build social solidarity among all Canadians and create a national identity that sticks. Every one of us, and especially those fortunate enough to be born in Canada, needs to shoulder some of the responsibility for reducing the barriers to integration that exist for newcomers. The fact that one in three immigrant families that came to Canada in the last five years currently lives at or near the poverty line is a national disgrace. It speaks volumes about the human cost of narrow social networks and the economic impact of low levels of social interaction between immigrant groups and mainstream society. It also suggests a fundamental deviation from our egalitarian roots and an unwholesome willingness to treat newcomers as a source of cheap manpower and dump them into the domestic labour pool whether there is real demand for their skills or not—and damn the social consequences for immigrants or the country as a whole.

We should acknowledge that our pride in being the world's largest per capita recipient of legal immigration carries with it real financial responsibilities. At a minimum, we should be prepared to spend on the citizenship acquisition and settlement processes—everything from ESL classes to job training to skills accreditation—the same per newcomer other high-immigration countries or almost double current expenditures. In reality, we should commit considerably more funds over the next five to ten years to repair the damage caused by decades of doing immigration on the cheap.

Furthermore, this money has to be distributed more equitably. The highly political agreements struck by the federal government with the provinces, especially those with Quebec, should be discarded. Instead, each province should receive a portion of increased federal funding for immigration settlement based on the number of new immigrants taking up residence in their jurisdiction.

Let's also use market forces to better equip newcomers by providing vouchers for services such as language training, skills upgrading and accreditation that are currently supplied by federally funded settlement agencies. Such vouchers would ensure that the dollars follow the newcomers and are not simply handed over to settlement support groups—many of which are funded because they serve specific ethnic constituencies and the political objectives of the government of the day. Vouchers could also create competition between big cities and smaller centres, encouraging immigrants to move to outlying communities where the services they desire, such as language and job training, are available at a lower cost. Delivering settlement funding where it is most needed is critical to building the social capital we know not only helps immigrants prosper but encourages them to put down roots.

There are no financial shortcuts to an efficient immigration system, unless we make significant reductions in the number of newcomers Canada accepts. But that choice is an economic non-starter: Canada will need increasingly higher levels of immigration to shore up its workforce. In sum, substantial new investments in our settlement systems and the citizenship acquisition process will be necessary if we want immigrants to thrive here and to take up the commitment of lifelong residency.

I am hopeful that we will wrap our minds around this simple truth in part because the price of failure is too great. Another two decades of misguided immigration and underfunded citizenship policies could create a vast immigrant underclass of individuals and families segregated in the congested corridors of the country's three or four sprawling megalopolises. What may save us from this fate is our belief in Canada's exceptionalism in the area of immigration. But we must act on this belief. If we fail to integrate these newcomers into an inclusive, economically rewarding and sustaining civic society, then we fail to achieve one of our singular claims to the world's attention and respect. We risk losing that flashing billboard that proclaims to the world: watch us and be amazed.

CITIZENSHIP AND THE CANADIAN-BORN

Newcomer or native-born, all Canadians will have to cope with the stresses of rapid social, ecological and economic changes. Responding to a host of new threats while maintaining a sense of social solidarity will not be easy for a society as divided as Canada's. Given these realities, I believe it is imperative that we place a new emphasis on citizenship for the Canadian-born.

Native-born Canadians must rid themselves of the spurious notion that assuming the responsibilities of citizenship—voting, knowing some Canadian history, volunteering, etc.—applies first and foremost to immigrants, that winning life's lottery and the prize of being born in Canada entitles its homegrown sons and daughters to generous, unconditional rights. It is time to recognize that native-born citizens cannot get away with token adherence to the kinds of social and economic responsibilities that newcomers are constantly being harangued for not embracing.

Mandatory Voting

The neglect of the responsibilities of citizenship has left us with the symptoms of civic decay in the body politic, chief among them plunging voting rates. As described earlier, not only have overall rates declined from a healthy 75 percent in the 1970s to a dismal 59 percent in the 2008 federal election, but each new cohort of eligible voters since the mid-1980s has turned out in fewer numbers than its predecessors. And the decline in the overall voting rate will only get worse as older, high-turnout voters dwindle in number.

There is more than a casual connection between casting a ballot at election time and Canada's ability to prepare itself to grapple with the implications of climate change or its fast-aging population. As political scientist Henry Milner correctly points out, voting "is the *sine qua non* of political participation. People who do not vote do not take part in more active forms of politics." In other words, much of the civic machinery—healthy political parties, sophisticated NGOs, grassroots activist groups—that our democratic society depends on to puzzle through complex social problems is intimately tied to that mysterious sense of political efficacy that leads us to a ballot box each election to cast our solitary vote.

In light of the well-documented links between voting and civic engagement, Canada should follow Australia's example and introduce mandatory voting. The Australian law is straightforward. Since 1924, every registered voter has been obliged to show up at a polling station on election day. Voters can spoil their ballots if they choose, but those who fail to appear receive a small fine in the mail. In the last national election, held as usual on a Saturday, when fewer people are working, over 90 percent of registered voters cast a ballot. In Canada, mandatory voting would not reverse poor turnouts in a single election. However, as in the case of reforming our lax citizenship laws, the principle of mandatory voting is important and, over time, could have a positive effect on Canadians' levels of overall political participation. It clearly has helped Australia maintain high levels of voter turnout during the very decades when other countries have witnessed steep declines in voting rates.

A National Civics Exam

The ills associated with plunging voter turnouts are closely associated with our abysmal knowledge of the country, especially its history and the workings of its democratic institutions. The forces that have turned us into a nation of amnesiacs are complex and numerous, ranging from the pervasive presence of American culture to the pull of strong regional identities to the erroneous, but deeply ingrained, belief that our history is boring.

That said, the neglect of Canadian history and civics in the schools has diminished our levels of civic literacy. It is unlikely that the governments of the seven Canadian provinces in which a course dedicated to Canadian history is not mandatory for graduation—among them the high-immigration jurisdictions of Alberta and British Columbia—will set aside their jealously guarded constitutional power over education and accept a federally dictated national curriculum. We need to come at this problem in a different way.

Instead of getting involved in the headaches of coordinating curricula across jurisdictions, what if the provincial ministries of education asked students to pass a civic literacy test to receive their high-school diploma—specifically the same exam that immigrants must take to become full citizens. Requiring every young person to take such an exam before they reach voting age or graduate from high school, whichever comes first, would make a powerful statement about the equal responsibilities of citizenship for all Canadians. It is also a popular idea among recent high-school graduates. Four out of five eighteen-to-twenty-five-year-olds surveyed by the Dominion Institute in 2007 supported the citizenship test as a requirement of graduation. Surely, if our young people are willing to set themselves to the task, a few enlightened provincial premiers could adopt this idea and begin the slow, but vital, process of improving Canadians' dismal civic literacy.

National Civic Service

Mandatory voting and a national civic literacy exam are relatively obvious ways to make citizenship more meaningful. But we can go further and draw lessons from our history on the deeper role of institutions and traditions that in the past have helped forge a common civic identity.

The issue of public education in Canada has fired debate since the early 1800s. For Joseph Howe and many of his generation, universal public education was vital not only to stimulate economic development but to knit together the colonies' sectarian factions and create bonds of loyalty to a broader civic culture. In Canada today, we are doing the opposite: dissociating the cultural and social challenges of high immigration from the need to provide young people of different ethnic, religious and socio-economic backgrounds with common educational experiences.

The statistics speak for themselves: enrollment in independent or private schools in Canada rose by 20 percent in the last decade. Privately funded religious schools have experienced a similar surge in popularity. Whereas the number of children attending publicly funded schools is much greater—nationally there are ten children in the public system for every one in private schools—some religious communities are sending their children to private religious institutions in significant numbers. For example, approximately 7 percent of Muslim children in Ontario currently attend private Islamic schools. Similarly high percentages of Jewish and Christian students attend private religious schools, and their numbers are increasing.

Perhaps more significant for the future of public education is the disproportionate number of wealthy Canadians who are taking their children out of the public system. Studies undertaken in the last decade show that only 5 percent or so of children from families with incomes less than $100,000 attend private schools. This flight of affluent families is driven by a number of factors, but anecdotal evidence from Canada's largest cities suggests that the impact of high immigration on the performance of public schools is a major cause. Whatever the reasons for this poor performance—the lack of language instructors to assist newly arrived youngsters or the behavioural problems associated with higher-than-average levels of poverty among the children of recent immigrants—many of the country's public schools are suffering the fallout of an underfunded immigration system.

Canadians need to wake up to the fact that there will be serious social repercussions if we segregate our children on the basis of wealth, religious belief or ethnicity. It is as vital in 2008 as it was a century and a half ago to forge social solidarity among ethnic groups and social classes and to maintain the egalitarian character of our country. But although urging the provinces to spend more on their public schools systems is worthwhile, it is not the whole answer, given that soaring health care costs are consuming an ever larger share of provincial budgets. Taxing private education to discourage parents from taking their children out of the public school system might help in some jurisdictions, but it is unlikely to significantly slow the exodus. The divisions in society threaten to reach into the classroom.

For all of these reasons, I think there is a compelling argument for the federal government to act and give life to an idea whose time has now come: a program of national civic service. Civic service to the community would share many of the same objectives of the public school systems established by our forebears to help create a common Canadian identity. A basic goal of a national service program would be to provide young people with a better understanding of Canada and each other.

Modelled on the successful national service schemes in countries as diverse as Denmark, Germany, Switzerland and Norway, such a program would require one-quarter of the approximately 400,000 young Canadians who turn eighteen each year to undertake eight months of service to their country. The 100,000 spots would be determined by national lottery. Selection by lottery is essential to ensure that young people from every region and a variety of ethnic and socio-economic backgrounds participate in the program. Although mandatory service would be controversial (in part a residue of Canada's troubled history with conscription), it represents an important principle: such an initiative would reinforce the core belief that Canadian citizenship involves real responsibilities not just for immigrants, but for all Canadians.

Participants in the program would have the opportunity to work in a wide range of areas: international aid, social work, the cultural industries, tutoring "at-risk" youth, caring for the sick and elderly and, yes, serving in the Canadian military. Ideally, the eight-month program would combine meaningful work and life experiences with travel in Canada and even abroad.

Such a program is not without precedent. Thirty years ago the federal government created Katimavik, the youth service program. In its first ten years, some 25,000 "Kat-kids" lived in rented communal houses in different parts of the country and performed a combination of volunteer social work and physical labour over the course of a nine-month program. One in ten participants could opt for the equivalent of military basic training, a feature of the program that was consistently oversubscribed. Kat-kids were paid a dollar a day and a $1,000 honorarium upon completion of the program. Although Katimavik was an undeniable success in its heyday, its potential was limited by a small annual intake: it accepted at most 5,000 participants per year, a number down to less than 1,000 today.

Certainly, such a scheme would require a significant outlay of public funds and might be opposed by many young people as an obstacle to their educational or career ambitions. But a far-sighted federal government could address these objections by using the program to advance another important policy objective: more equitable access to post-secondary education. Every young person selected for national service would be entitled to a financial subsidy equal to the cost of three years of higher or continuing education at the institution of their choice. Since more than half of all Canadian university and college students graduate with, on average, a whopping $24,000 in education-related debt, such a pledge would make national service a rewarding opportunity that would help young people pursue their future ambitions. This would be especially true for participants from lower-income families who would benefit from easier access to post-secondary education.

The other major costs associated with operating a large-scale program of national service would include a central coordinating body and a monthly cash stipend for each participant. If the objective was to "graduate" 100,000 young people per year, the total annual price tag for the program could be as high as $4 billion. To put this into context, the federal government's program spending averages $200 billion a year. The cost of a civic service scheme would represent 2 percent of total federal expenditures—a not unreasonable $121 from every Canadian.

It is important to note that in countries that have national youth service initiatives both the not-for-profit sector and local governments share in the program's costs. Everyone benefits from the creation of millions of hours of free manpower that can be used to support and maintain worthy programs and institutions. This would be doubly true for provincial governments, which would also benefit from the tuition subsidy the new program would provide to a sizable portion of the 100,000 annual graduates of the mandatory eight-month civic service scheme.

Beyond the immediate social advantages that could flow from a large-scale civic service program—increased social capital, a strengthened volunteer sector, greater knowledge of the country's regions and a mixing of ethnic and socio-economic groups—there is the opportunity to reaffirm and enhance young people's sense of belonging to the larger national enterprise called Canada. Bonds of attachment between Canadians and their national government may prove to be vital assets when the country faces issues requiring national action and individual sacrifice. More optimistically, such a scheme could generate the commitment to larger purpose and the impetus to nation building that infused the country in the aftermath of the Second World War—the last time large numbers of Canadians mobilized around a common cause and changed the country for the better.

ALL TOGETHER NOW

My vision for a revitalized Canadian citizenship that carries real obligations for newcomers and native-born alike will not prevent global warming or slow the aging of Canadian society. Although there are obvious connections between reinvesting in our shared citizenship and making high levels of immigration work for newcomers and the country as a whole, Canadians have shown little inclination, so far, to connect these dots and overhaul both institutions. It also needs to be acknowledged that there are some Canadians who will have nothing to do with a state-led reassertion of citizenship. Aboriginal peoples in particular have strongly felt allegiances to entities that predate Canada's existence, and many regard their Canadian citizenship as secondary to who they are as individuals and nations.

On this point let me be clear: my enthusiasm for a revitalized shared citizenship and the prescriptions I have put forward are not aimed at homogenizing Canadian society or rolling back the clock to the 1950s or the 1840s when entire groups where excluded from the mainstream. Rather, my objective is to reaffirm a core set of obligations that we owe to each other, so that Canada maintains the national institutions and small-l liberal values that allow us, with all our dissimilarities, to coexist.

As a people we have long understood the necessity to balance whatever exclusive claims we might be tempted to make on behalf of some "group identity" with the need to support institutions that allow our differences to flourish. It was this proclivity that produced responsible government and brought together the coalition of French and English Reformers who established the democratic framework of our society. It was also the rationale behind much of the nation building in postwar Canada, such as universal health insurance, old-age pensions and equalization. It is the cultural attitude that lives on in our thinking about citizenship and what we owe each other and Canada.

Viewed through the lens of a reinvigorated citizenship, Canada's prospects appear to me far more optimistic. An enhanced Canadian citizenship that is founded on meaningful and reciprocal responsibilities resonates with the best of who we are as a people. For starters, it provides a way to channel our long-standing aversion to sectarianism into a positive and potentially inspiring common project and away from the "us versus them" attitude that is increasingly colouring our debates about immigration and multiculturalism.

Next, policies such as instituting a civic literacy exam, mandatory voting and a national civic service afford the opportunity to renew, in our own era, our forebears' century-and-a-half-long commitment to public education and the belief in the centrality of state institutions to help inculcate a shared identity and affirm the egalitarian character of Canadian democracy and our society as a whole.

Similarly, longer residency requirements for newcomers and an end to obligation-free dual citizenship are ideas intimately embedded in our political DNA. We are a nation in which one's commitment to the country has traditionally mattered as much as it does in the great revolutionary democracy to the south. We are a settler country whose civic identity is based on the idea that full citizenship is not defined by race or social class, but instead earned through physical residence and contribution to the life and institutions of one's local community.

Citizenship matters, too, in the context of our latest experiment in Canadian exceptionalism vis-à-vis our peer nations: sustaining the highest per capita levels of legal immigration in the world. To fail in this task is to lose not only global bragging rights and strong economic prospects, but our self-confidence that we are an ambitious country capable of great achievements.

In addition, citizenship provides those of us who resist the siren call of the "postnational" state with a redoubt from which to fight for the idea that what gives our individual existence depth and texture is participation in a public life of larger meaning, a rich and robust civic community that transcends our linguistic, regional and ethnic differences.

Finally, a vision of Canadian citizenship that includes substantive civic obligations could prove essential to replenishing our depleted reserves of social solidarity—the civic literacy and social capital that our society needs to function smoothly—so that we can meet head-on the forces that will inevitably transform our world and Canada.

8 | A CONFESSION AND A PROPOSAL

AFTER admonishing my readers to assume the responsibilities and duties of Canadian citizenship, I need to make a personal confession. I am a citizen of Canada and of the United Kingdom of Great Britain and Northern Ireland. Yes, despite my conviction that dual citizenship devalues Canadian citizenship, I am one of the more than 3.5 million Canadian citizens who hold a second passport.

My United Kingdom passport entitles me to vote in British elections, attend, at subsidized cost, some of the world's finest universities and, should I wish, leave Canada to work and live in the United Kingdom hassle-free. In addition, my British citizenship bestows on me all of the rights of full membership in the European Community. I could conceivably take up residency in Italy, vote for the next president of Slovenia or accept a job with the Académie française. And like all dual citizens, I can confer all of the benefits of my UK citizenship on my children and spouse.

These practical advantages aside, my status as a British and European citizen has one additional perk. There is something undeniably impressive about the dynamism of Europe today and the fact that half a billion Europeans are succeeding in fashioning a civic identity that encompasses twenty-seven member states, twenty-three languages and a $17 trillion economy. The public architecture sprouting up in the continent's capitals, the wealth of culture and history that is part of Europeans' day-to-day lives and the growth of a pan-European culture that fuses the modern and the traditional in counterpoint to American-style consumerism are exciting and inspiring. In not so subtle ways my British passport represents a kind of standing invitation, should things not work out for me in Canada, to become a participant in one of the world's great social, political and economic experiments.

Notwithstanding the allure of Europe, my decision in my mid-twenties to become a dual citizen was made for sentimental rather than practical reasons. Family history and a desire to acknowledge that the choices my parents and grandparents made had shaped my own life led me to claim a second citizenship. My experience makes me believe most dual citizens do not possess a second citizenship for lifestyle reasons, to have an at-the-ready licence to work, live and play in another country. Rather, the motivation to acquire or retain a second citizenship has strong emotional undercurrents. It is a way to stay connected to the people, places and events beyond Canada that people imagine contributed to the sum of who they are as individuals. Quite naturally, this feeling is strongest among recent newcomers. If you have first-hand memories of your childhood neighbourhood, the house you grew up in or a much-loved relative—all removed from you by time and space—your second citizenship acts as a kind of covenant to remember where you came from and what you left behind.

Nonetheless, I was surprised when I learned that there are as many as 750,000 people like me, who were born in Canada but have acquired the citizenship of another country. According to an Ipsos Reid poll conducted in 2007, this group comprises one in every thirty-three Canadian adults and is highly educated and financially well off. Its members do not come overwhelmingly from Quebec, the one province where one might expect larger numbers of Canadian-born citizens to maintain a second citizenship for reason of culture, but rather they are distributed proportionately across the country. Canadian-born dual citizens constitute a not insignificant segment of Canadian society.

In the course of researching and writing this book, I started to question my decision to acquire a second citizenship. In fact, I started to feel increasingly uncomfortable about the emotional trade-offs that dual citizenship involves. Yes, my decision to apply for a British passport was motivated by family considerations, not by my desire to live abroad. Like many Canadians, I spent some time living overseas in the 1990s, and the experience convinced me that Canada was my permanent home. But equally, I could not deny the thoughts that arose at the back of my mind once I had British citizenship. It encouraged a rich fantasy life about what my future might hold, a life more adventurous, ambitious or lucrative than my current prospects in Canada seemed to promise. If I was frustrated by congestion and pollution in my native Toronto, I could fantasize about pulling up stakes and going to join my sister in pastoral and pristine rural Italy. When I was disillusioned about the Dominion Institute and doubting that we were making a difference, I would daydream about a new career in Berlin or Paris. During the Québécois-as-a-nation debate, I remember thinking that if the federal government had decided to recognize a new class of Canadian citizen to which I could never belong, maybe Europe and its effort to forge a true partnership of twenty-seven nationalities was my philosophical home. In effect, my second passport had become a licence to second-guess the decisions I was making in my daily life and to ponder how, if future circumstances warranted, I might make a fresh start free of the frustrations that being Canadian can entail.

But I have come to the conclusion that Canada will not survive the coming century if more and more of its Canadian-born citizens continue to live, as I have, with the mental gymnastics of dual citizenship. As I have argued, the scale and complexity of the challenges Canada will face are like nothing we have experienced in living memory. When the effects of our fast-aging population and of climate change begin to hit home—starting in 2020 and then intensifying relentlessly as we move towards the mid-century mark—Canadians' collective flight or fight instincts will kick in. Those of us who choose to fight will respond to the social stresses wracking our society with a spirit of solidarity and self-sacrifice. Others, driven by the flight instinct, will act out of self-interest and self-preservation. Which of these two instincts ultimately triumphs depends, in no small part, on how we each imagine our place in Canada.

In my case, the experience of living in Canada as a dual citizen undeniably introduced an element of doubt as to whether my allegiances to the country are, in fact, unconditional. Who is to say that after living for another decade in a Canada struggling to cope with rapid ecological, economic and social change, I will not end up finding a convenient rationale to justify leaving for England's "green and pleasant land"?

I believe that each of us, whether our families have been here for generations or only a few years, needs to decide that this country, Canada, is where we will make our collective stand. If we are to not just survive, but thrive as a people in the century ahead, we must acknowledge that there is no opting out, no à la carte menu of rights and responsibilities and no bolthole we can escape through when the going gets tough. We have to realize, and quickly, that among the first casualties of the challenging times ahead are our assumptions about how little we can owe each other and Canada and still get by as a country. All of us will be called upon to make prolonged, and at times painful, sacrifices that will involve relinquishing entitlements that we consider "rights." This will be especially difficult for the country's elites who are not rooted in Canada by a strong sense of history or place and who assess the value of citizenship in terms of the access it provides to the highest quality of life possible for the fewest obligations.

We have to shake off the faulty reasoning that the absence of widely shared civic values and robust national institutions is responsible for our success in an era of globalization and social change. Instead, we need to remember, once again, to be loyal to ourselves. We must commit ourselves, as our forebears did in the 1840s and the 1950s, to creating institutions and reinforcing values that forge bonds of allegiance with each other and express the reality of who we are as a people. At all costs, we must not revert to the colonial mindset that dual citizenship encourages, the corrosive attitude that imagines that life in the great imperial cities of Washington, Paris or London is somehow more real and more consequential than life in Canada.

These thoughts bring me to my final policy prescription: Canada should return to a version of the pre-1977 practice of annulling the citizenship of Canadian adults who voluntarily and formally acquire the citizenship of another country. In our present era, this law should apply only to natural-born citizens, whether living inside or outside the country, who have at least one parent who is a Canadian citizen. Exceptions would be made for people who assume a second citizenship through adoption or marriage, and for newcomers. This law would have two objectives. It would seek to impress on the Canadian-born that there is no opt-out clause in their social contract with Canada. It is up to those of us who were lucky enough to be born Canadian to take on our share of the hard work that will be required to see the country through whatever demands the coming century holds. Its other objective would be to let all aspiring citizens know that assuming Canadian citizenship has an important, permanent and unavoidable consequence: the children you have once you become a citizen can and will only be Canadian.

I have come to believe strongly in the "in for a penny, in for a pound" sentiment that comes with having a single citizenship, especially in high-immigration countries such as Canada. It creates the impetus for each of us to become more politically active, to get involved in our local communities and to learn something about the country and each other. The virtuous circle that creates higher rates of social capital and civic literacy is fueled in no small part by a healthy dose of self-interest—our understanding that the way of life we enjoy day in and day out depends on each of us giving back to the community and to the country as a whole.

That said, I do not believe it is reasonable to mandate that newcomers to Canada renounce the citizenship of their homelands. There can be no doubt that they feel far more pressure to retain a second citizenship than the Canadian-born. For first-generation immigrants, a second passport can help ensure that they can visit their extended families unimpeded and, should they wish, keep up business relationships that are integral to their livelihood in Canada and the larger economy.

But for the three-quarters of a million Canadian-born adults who voluntarily became dual citizens plus the millions of second-generation Canadians that will be born in the coming decades—most of whom will be legally entitled to claim a second citizenship—the time has come to acknowledge that the practice of dual citizenship does a disservice to the country that gives us so much and asks so little in return. We are needlessly assuming conflicting loyalties, weakening the bonds of solidarity and common purpose that hold the country together and perpetuating a minimalist vision of what we owe each other and Canada. Canadians are also being highly hypocritical when we demand that newcomers adopt "Canadian values" while at the same time embracing a system that allows generation after generation of Canadian-born to hedge their bets on whether Canada is, in fact, their permanent home. In the end, dual citizenship erodes the confidence of this diverse and decentralized nation that we are all committed to making work regardless of the obstacles we face.

In their hearts Canadian-born dual citizens recognize these contradictions and are aware that we need to make this first and comparatively tiny sacrifice in order to perpetuate a way of life we have all benefitted from immeasurably. Let us once and for all cast off the security blanket of dual citizenship and embrace, in the manner of our forebears, this project called Canada—unreservedly, irrevocably and most of all passionately.

| ACKNOWLEDGEMENTS

THIS book is very much the product of the people and ideas that inspired the work of the Dominion Institute. I owe a special debt of gratitude to Allan Gotlieb, the Chair of the Donner Canadian Foundation. Not only was the Donner Foundation instrumental in launching the Institute, its ongoing support provided me with the opportunity, as executive director, to immerse myself in the debates, issues and ideas I have explored in this book.

Equally inspiring have been the writings of, the conversations with and the personal encouragement from authors Andrew Cohen, Jack Granatstein, Richard Gwyn and John Ralston Saul. All of them have contributed immeasurably to Canadians' efforts to reimagine their country through a greater understanding of its past, and they have done so with care, insight and wit. I also want to thank three close friends for the thoughtful advice and litany of ideas which are peppered through this book: Antony Anderson, Michael David Chong and Giles Gherson.

As a first-time author, little did I know just how time-consuming writing a book would be. My dear friend Erik Penz, the Dominion Institute's chair, helped organize an extended leave, allowing me to write full-time. Alison Faulknor assumed the day-to-day running of the Institute in my absence and oversaw all of the work of the organization with great aplomb. My inestimable editor, Jan Walter, stoically endured my first-time writer's nerves; her experience, skill and steady hand are evident throughout the manuscript. I also want to thank my publisher, Scott McIntyre, for acquiring *Who We Are* and for his sage counsel. It is an honour to be published by the largest Canadian-owned publisher in the country. Here, too, Michael A. Levine and Westwood Creative Artists, my agents, should be singled out for their championing of Canadian writers and non-fiction books on Canadian themes.

. . .

There are three more people who warrant special thanks. The first are my parents, Franklyn Griffiths and Meg Hogarth. They saw me through my struggle with dyslexia as a child and instilled in me a love of books and all things Canadian. The other, who more than anyone else supported me through the process of researching and writing this book, is my wife and partner, Jennifer Lambert. Quite simply, without her patience and loving advice, *Who We Are* would not have been written.

| NOTES

| INTRODUCTION

p. xii One in three Canadians surveyed....
Dominion Institute, "Annual Canada Day Survey, 2007," 30 June 2007,
http://www.dominion.ca/polling.htm (accessed 12 September 2008).

I | NATION OR NOTION?

p. 1 Invoking visionaries of the past....
Stephen Harper, "The Québécois," in Canada, Parliament, House of
Commons, *Debates* (Hansard), 141:84 (22 November 2006), 5198.

p. 2 Next to rise was the interim leader....
Bill Graham, "The Québécois," in Canada, Parliament, House of Commons, *Debates* (Hansard), 141:84 (22 November 2006), 5199.

p. 4 Commenting on his motion to the media....
Allan Woods, "Bloc Back Harper's Quebec Motion: Nation Status,"
Vancouver Sun, 25 November 2006, A8.

p. 5 To the *Globe and Mail*'s John Ibbitson....
John Ibbitson, "Nobody Saw This Coming—Nobody," *Globe and Mail*,
23 November 2006, A1.

p. 6 In the words of the prime minister....
Robert Dutrisac, "Harper Courts Québec," *Le Devoir*,
20 December 2005, A1.

p. 6 Influential Calgary-based commentator....
Barry Cooper, "Au revoir, Trudeau Era," *Calgary Herald*, 29 November
2006, A20.

p. 8   The challenge that has long stood....
         Thomas D'Arcy McGee, "A Canadian Nationality," in *Great Canadian Speeches,* ed. Dennis Gruending, 30.

p. 9   Journalist Andrew Coyne correctly excoriated....
         Andrew Coyne, "And with That, We're on Our Way to Belgiumhood," *National Post,* 23 November 2006, A1.

p. 9   But our larger objection was....
         John George Lambton Durham, *Lord Durham's Report on the Affairs of British North America,* 16.

p. 9   Whether it was the alliance....
         Somewhere in the order of 25,000 French Canadians served in the Great War and another 150,000 in the Second World War. With an average casualty rate of 7 percent between the two wars, it is conceivable that 5,000 or more French Canadians perished in both conflicts.

p. 11   According to the Centre for the Study of Democracy....
         Thomas Axworthy, "Money, Money Everywhere...But They're Giving away the Store," *Globe and Mail,* 20 March 2007, A31.

p. 12   Bliss opposed the motion....
         Michael Bliss, "Canada under Attack," *National Post,* 25 November 2006, A1.

p. 13   As constitutional veteran Roy Romanow....
         Roy Romanow and John Whyte, "Stephen Harper Traded the Peaceable Kingdom for a Trojan Horse," *Globe and Mail,* 8 December 2006, A25.

p. 14   Our predecessors spent a significant part....
         Michael J. Sandel, *Public Philosophy,* 2.

p. 14   For Bloc leader Gilles Duceppe....
         Gilles Duceppe, "The Québécois," in Canada, Parliament, House of Commons, *Debates* (Hansard), 141:86 (24 November 2006), 5305.

p. 15   According to public opinion polls....
         Leger Marketing, "For 67% of Canadians, Québec is Not a Nation," 29 November 2006, http://www.legermarketing.com (accessed 1 January 2008).

p. 15   To quote a letter published....
         John Lorinc, "Here We Go Again...," *Globe and Mail,* 24 November 2006, A24.

p. 16   Add to that, as journalist Richard Gywn put it....
         Richard Gwyn, *Rediscovering Our Citizenship,* 3.

p. 17   It is not simply that we have....
         $100,000 is the amount of revenue the federal government accrues from

the interest on holding the investor applicant's $400,000 refundable deposit for a five-year period.

p. 18 In the words of historian Desmond Morton....
Desmond Morton, "Divided Loyalties? Divided Country?," in *Belonging*, ed. William Kaplan, 62.

p. 19 In the majority of our school systems....
J.L. Granatstein, *Who Killed Canadian History?*, 158.

p. 19 In 2007, a national survey....
Dominion Institute, "What Do Young Adults Know About Canadian History?: A Ten Year Bench Mark Study," November 2007, http://www.dominion.ca/polling.htm (accessed 12 September 2008).

p. 20 We know from prestigious publications....
Economist Intelligence Unit, "Not Left Behind: How Canada Can Compete," *Economist*, March 2007, 5.

p. 22 As one commentator correctly surmised....
Andrew Coyne, "Seeking a Grand Bargain," *National Post*, 12 May 2007, A20.

p. 22 In 2007, just before the onset....
Crosbie & Company, "M&A Reports," 2007, http://www.crosbieco.com (accessed 12 September 2008).

p. 23 According to Roger Martin....
Roger Martin and Gordon Nixon, "A Prescription for Canada: Rethink Our Tax Policy," *Globe and Mail*, 1 July 2007, B1.

p. 24 At the time, the Dominion Institute....
The Memory Project, "Oral History of Charles Laking," November 2004, http://www.thememoryproject.com/digital-archive/ (accessed 12 September 2008).

p. 25 Still, he was extremely proud....
Brian Whitwham, "Great War a Horror Not to Be Forgotten," *Guelph Mercury*, 11 November 2005, R2.

p. 25 In every way Charles was an exemplary Canadian....
Jennifer Campbell, "WWI Veteran Saw Action in France: Clare Laking," *National Post*, 28 November 2005, A4.

2 | THE UNENCUMBERED COUNTRY

p. 29 For political scientist John Kirton....
John Kirton, "Canada Shows Its Strength," *Toronto Star*, 31 October 2006, A21.

p. 29　The rest of the country has picked up....
　　　Dominion Institute, "Canada in 2020," 30 June 2006, http://www.dominion
　　　.ca/polling.htm (accessed 12 September 2008).

p. 30　After praising Canada as a great place....
　　　Michael Higgins, "Montreal Author Wins Booker Prize," *National Post*,
　　　23 October 2002, A3.

p. 31　Richard Gwyn quipped....
　　　Richard Gywn, "PM Should Heed Governor General," *Toronto Star*,
　　　14 October 2005, A29.

p. 31　Journalist and author Andrew Cohen....
　　　Andrew Cohen, *The Unfinished Canadian*, 160–1.

p. 32　To quote philosopher John Ralston Saul....
　　　John Ralston Saul, "The Way We Are: Canada Is a World Leader in the
　　　Great Experiment of Immigration," *Vancouver Sun*, 28 February 2007, A17.

p. 33　In the words of globalization enthusiast Pico Iyer....
　　　Pico Iyer, *The Global Soul*, 34.

p. 33　Poet and essayist B.W. Powe sums up....
　　　B.W. Powe, *Towards a Canada of Light*, 123.

p. 35　As social commentator Allan Gregg put it....
　　　Allan Gregg, *The Big Picture*, 52.

p. 35　It is remarkable that in a country....
　　　William Cross and Lisa Young, "The Shifting Place of Political Parties in
　　　Canadian Public Life," *Choices*, 12:4, 17.

p. 36　Electoral returns show....
　　　Centre for Research and Information on Canada (CRIC), "Citizen Partici-
　　　pation and Canadian Democracy: An Overview," Montreal: CRIC, 2003.

p. 36　With participation rates for first-time voters....
　　　For a concise explanation of why Election Canada's estimates of 38 percent
　　　first-time voter turnout in recent federal elections is overly optimistic,
　　　see Henry Milner, "Are Young Canadians Becoming Political Dropouts?,"
　　　Choices, 11:3, 3–4.

p. 36　Also striking, the same studies reveal....
　　　World Values Survey, "Online Data Analysis," 1981–2004, http://
　　　www.worldvaluessurvey.org (accessed 12 September 2008).

p. 37　Between 1990 and 2007, roughly the same....
　　　Dominion Institute, "2007 Canada Day Survey," 30 June 2007, http://
　　　www.dominion.ca/polling.htm (accessed 12 September 2008).

p. 37   Peter C. Newman described the shift this way....
         Peter C. Newman, *Defining Moments*, 244.

p. 38   According to comprehensive studies....
         Statistics Canada, 2003 General Social Survey on Social Engagement, Cycle 17:
         An Overview of Findings (Ottawa: Statistics Canada, 2004), No. 89–598–XIE.

p. 39   In a 2005 Dominion Institute survey....
         Peter Evans, "Diversity, Freedoms Make Us Unique," *National Post*,
         24 September 2005, A22.

p. 40   In a survey the Dominion Institute conducted in 2007....
         Dominion Institute, "Becoming Canadian Survey," 2 March 2007,
         http://www.dominion.ca/polling.htm (accessed 12 September 2008).

p. 42   Robert Putnam, the political scientist....
         Robert D. Putnam, "Bowling Alone: America's Declining Social Capital,"
         Journal of Democracy, 6:1 (January 1995), 71.

p. 43   But according to detailed analyses....
         This section draws on research conducted by Paul B. Reed and Kevin
         Selbee for "The Civic Core in Canada: Disproportionality in Charitable
         Giving, Volunteering, and Civic Participation," *Nonprofit and Voluntary
         Sector Quarterly*, 30:4 (2001), 761–76.

p. 44   It is worth remembering....
         Barbara Righton, "How We Live," *Maclean's*, 1 July 2006, 41.

p. 45   It is not surprising that....
         See Martin Turcotte, "Time Spent with Family on a Typical Workday,
         1986 to 2005," Canadian Social Trends, Vol. 83 (2007).

p. 45   At the Dominion Institute we were surprised....
         Dominion Institute. "Becoming Canadian Survey," 2 March 2007,
         http://www.dominion.ca/polling.htm (accessed 12 September 2008).

p. 45   As Robert Putnam discovered to his chagrin....
         Robert D. Putnam, "E Pluribus Unum: Diversity and Community
         in the Twenty-first Century: The 2006 Johan Skytte Prize Lecture,"
         Scandinavian Political Studies, 30:2 (2007), 137–74.

p. 46   Australians and Americans are twice as likely....
         World Values Survey, "Online Data Analysis," 1981–2004, http://
         www.worldvaluessurvey.org (accessed 12 September 2008).

p. 47   For instance, in 2001 the Dominion Institute....
         Dominion Institute, "5th Annual Canada Day Survey," 29 June 2001,
         http://www.dominion.ca/polling.htm (accessed 12 September 2008).

p. 48   When presented in 2002 with fifty-odd questions....
        National Geographic, "National Geographic–Roper 2002 Global
        Geographic Literacy Survey," http://www.nationalgeographic.com
        (accessed 12 September 2008).

p. 48   One last finding....
        Dominion Institute, "Mock-Citizenship Exam," 29 June 2007,
        http://www.dominion.ca/polling.htm (accessed 12 September 2008).

3 | FUTURE SHOCKS

p. 56   To quote Université du Québec economist Pierre Fortin....
        Pierre Fortin, "The Baby Boomers' Tab: Already $40 Billion in 2020,"
        in *Canada in 2020*, ed. Rudyard Griffiths, 44–5.

p. 56   In British Columbia, for example....
        Gary Mason, "B.C. Health Care's 'Very, Very Scary' Future," *Globe and Mail*,
        12 February 2007, A6.

p. 57   Unfortunately for many modern industrial nations....
        David Foot, "A Fortunate Country," in *Canada in 2020*, ed. Rudyard Griffiths,
        149–58.

p. 59   Indeed, studies do show....
        This section draws on research conducted by Yvan Guillemette and
        William B.P. Robson for their paper "No Elixir of Youth: Immigration Can-
        not Keep Canada Young," *C.D. Howe Institute Backgrounder*, No. 96 (2006).

p. 60   According to the 2006 census data....
        Tina Chui, Keely Tran and Hélène Maheux, *Immigration in Canada: A Portrait
        of the Foreign-born Population, 2006 Census* (Ottawa: Statistics Canada, 2004),
        No. 97–557–XIE.

p. 60   Research shows conclusively....
        Statistics Canada, Report on the Demographic Situation in Canada
        (Ottawa: Statistics Canada, 2006), No. 89–598–XIE, 105; Library of Parlia-
        ment, *Canada's Immigration Program (Background Paper)* (Ottawa:
        Parliamentary Research and Information Service, 2004), BP–109E, 7–8.

p. 61   Economists calculate we would need....
        Yvan Guillemette and William B.P. Robson, "No Elixir of Youth: Immigration
        Cannot Keep Canada Young," *C.D. Howe Institute Backgrounder*, No. 96 (2006).

p. 61   This trend is already evident in cities....
        James Rusk, "Suburbs Outpacing Toronto in Population Growth,"
        Globe and Mail, 14 March 2007, A14.

p. 61   Recent studies show....
         Statistics Canada, *Earnings and Income of Canadians Over the Last
         Quarter Century, 2006 Census* (Ottawa: Statistics Canada, 2006),
         No. 97–563–XIE, 44.

p. 62   If we look ahead to a future....
         Daniel Stoffman, "Sao Paulo of the North: The Effects of Mass Immigration,"
         in *Canada in 2020*, ed. Rudyard Griffiths, 29.

p. 64   Since the scientific measurement of global temperatures....
         R. K. Pachauri and A. Reisinger, *Climate Change 2007*, 104.

p. 65   By 2012, their total combined emissions....
         Mark Clayton, "New Coal Plants Bury 'Kyoto'," *Christian Science Monitor*,
         23 December 2004, A1; Fareed Zakaria, "The Case for a Global Carbon
         Tax," *Newsweek International*, 16 April 2007, 17.

p. 67   It has been suggested....
         Andrew C. Revkin, "As China Goes, So Goes Global Warming," *New York
         Times*, 16 December 2007, WK3.

p. 67   This is the danger zone....
         Stern Review Report, "Executive Summary (long)," 30 October 2006,
         http://www.hm-treasury.gov.uk/ (accessed 12 September 2008).

p. 67   For Canada, higher average temperatures....
         Canadian Council of Ministers of the Environment, *Climate, Nature and
         People: Indicators of Canada's Climate Change* (Ottawa: CCME, 2003), 40; Peter
         Calamai, "Climate Forecast Grim for Canada," *Toronto Star*, 2 April 2007, A6;
         Allan Woods, "Damage to Forest Changes Kyoto Equation," *Toronto Star*, 4
         April 2007, A4.

p. 69   One can imagine a new "green divide"....
         Kirk Makin, "Clash over Oil Sands Inevitable: Lougheed," *Globe and Mail*,
         http://www.globeandmail.com (accessed 12 September 2008); Roger
         Gibbins, "The Curse of Alberta," in *Canada in 2020*, ed. Rudyard Griffiths,
         67–74.

p. 70   With some 70 percent of all immigrants....
         Citizenship and Immigration Canada, "The Monitor: Third Quarter Data
         2006," http://www.cic.gc.ca (accessed 12 September 2008).

4 | PASSAGE TO CANADA

p. 74   My own views about immigration....
         See Rudyard Griffiths, ed., *Passages*.

p. 79   In the words of John Ralston Saul....
        John Ralston Saul, "The Way We Are: Canada Is a World Leader in the
        Great Experiment of Immigration," *Vancouver Sun*, 28 February 2007, A17.

p. 79   On average, Canada welcomes....
        See the OECD Factbook 2008, http:// www.oecd.org (accessed
        12 September 2008).

p. 80   Over the past twenty years....
        Statistics Canada, Immigration in Canada: A Portrait of the Foreign-
        born Population, 2006 Census (Ottawa: Statistics Canada, 2006),
        No. 97–557–XIE, 7–9.

p. 80   Canada's status as an immigration superpower....
        Lisa Benton-Short, Marie D. Price and Samantha Friedman, "Globalization
        from Below," *International Journal of Urban and Regional Research*, 29:4
        (December 2005), 945–59.

p. 81   Consider the international surveys....
        Simon Anholt, *Anholt Nation Brands Index Summary Data Q4 2007*,
        http://www.earthspeak.com (accessed 12 September 2008).

p. 81   In Asian surveys, Canadians are judged....
        Ron Richardson and Jim Storey, "Canada's Brand: Clean and Friendly,"
        National Post, 12 October 2000, C19.

p. 82   In recent years, upwards of 84 percent....
        Irene Bloemraad, "Becoming a Citizen in the United States and Canada:
        Structured Mobilization and Immigrant Political Incorporation, *Social
        Forces*, 85:1 (December 2006), 667–95.

p. 82   The Dominion Institute found in 2007....
        Dominion Institute, "Mock-Citizenship Exam," 29 June 2007,
        http://www.dominion.ca/polling.htm (accessed 12 September 2008).

p. 83   The percentage of recent immigrants....
        Statistics Canada, *Earnings and Income of Canadians Over the Last Quarter Cen-
        tury, 2006 Census* (Ottawa: Statistics Canada, 2006), No. 97–563–XIE, 44.

p. 84   The increase in poverty....
        This section draws on Statistics Canada, *The Rise in Low-Income Rates
        Among Immigrants in Canada* (Ottawa: Statistics Canada, 2003),
        No. 11F0019MIE, 1–58.

p. 84   The percentage of new immigrants....
        Marina Jiménez, "Immigrants Battle Chronic Low Income," *Globe and
        Mail*, 31 January 2007, A5.

p. 84 Immigrants living in poverty....
Statistics Canada, *Intergenerational Educational Mobility Among the Children of Canadian Immigrants* (Ottawa: Statistics Canada, 2008), No. 316–11F0019M, 18.

p. 85 Multi-generational research shows....
Stephen P. Jenkins and Thomas Siedler, "The intergenerational transmission of poverty in industrialized countries," CPRC *Working Paper 75*, (April 2007), 4–5.

p. 85 For instance, one long-term study of Canadian children....
D. Ross and P. Roberts, Income and Child Well-Being: A New Perspective on the Poverty Debate (Ottawa: Canadian Council on Social Development, 1999), 52.

p. 85 It certainly does not help immigrant children....
Jill Mahoney, "More Than Half of ESL Students without Specialist Teachers," *Globe and Mail*, 2 May 2007, A9.

p. 86 Unequal and highly politically federal funding....
Alan Broadbent, *Urban Nation*, 181.

p. 87 The sources of Canadian immigration....
Tina Chui, Keely Tran and Hélène Maheux, *Immigration in Canada: A Portrait of the Foreign-born Population, 2006 Census* (Ottawa: Statistics Canada, 2004), No. 97–557–XIE, 9–11.

p. 87 According to an exhaustive study....
Jeffery G. Reitz and Rupa Banerjee, "Racial Inequality, Social Cohesion and Policy Issues in Canada," in *Belonging?*, eds. Keith Banting, Thomas Courchene and Leslie Seidle, 497.

p. 87 This compares to one in ten white immigrants....
Dominion Institute, "Anti Racism Survey," 21 March 2005, http://www.dominion.ca/polling.htm (accessed 12 September 2008).

p. 88 The breadth and depth of this racial divide....
Jeffery G. Reitz and Rupa Banerjee, "Racial Inequality, Social Cohesion and Policy Issues in Canada," in *Belonging?*, eds. Keith Banting, Thomas Courchene and Leslie Seidle, 505–19.

p. 89 The number of ethnic enclaves in Canada....
Margaret Wente, "254 Solitudes, and Counting," *Globe and Mail*, 30 June 2007, A15.

p. 90 This social fragmentation became clear to me....
Dominion Institute, "Becoming Canadian Survey," 2 March 2007, http://www.dominion.ca/polling.htm (accessed 12 September 2008).

p. 92 Also, unlike Europeans and Americans....

Ipsos Reid, "Canada: A Land of Immigrants Becomes More Positive about Immigration," 16 June 2007, http://www.ipsos.ca (accessed 12 September 2008).

p. 93 Despite a Canadian contribution of less than two hundred troops....

United Nations, "Monthly Summary of Contributions of Military and Civilian Police Personnel," http://www.un.org/ (accessed 12 September 2008).

5 | FIRST PRINCIPLES

p. 98 The powerful emotion of loyalty....

This section draws on David Mills' excellent book *The Idea of Loyalty in Upper Canada, 1784–1850* and an essay I wrote for *Historic Kingston* entitled "Ambition and Loyalty: The Making of John A. Macdonald and Confederation," Vol. 54 (2006), 2-17.

p. 99 According to historian S.F. Wise....

S.F. Wise, "Colonial Attitudes from 1812 to 1837," in *Canada Views the United States*, ed. S.F. Wise (Seattle: University of Washington Press, 1967), 22.

p. 101 As arch-conservative John Strachan put it....

John Strachan, *A Discourse on the Character of King George the Third*, 43.

p. 101 In the words of the British general and hero....

Quoted in S.D. Clark, *Movements in Protest in Canada, 1640–1840* (Toronto: University of Toronto Press, 1959), 220.

p. 101 As one arch-Tory vowed at the time....

Quoted in Francis Collins, *An Abridged View of the Alien Question Unmasked* (York: Canadian Freeman, 1826).

p. 103 This sentiment comes through....

See *Farmers Journal*, 26 November 1828.

p. 105 Historian Desmond Morton dates the beginning....

Desmond Morton, "Divided Loyalties? Divided Country?," in *Belonging*, ed. William Kaplan, 54.

p. 107 Historian Allan Greer points out....

Allan Greer, *The Patriots and the People*, 117.

p. 107 In Upper Canada, the march....

Charles Anderson, *Bluebloods and Rednecks*, 165.

p. 108 Of the 111 men charged with high treason....

For a powerful first-person account of the hardships French Canadians endured in Australia's penal colonies, see Francois-Maurice Lepailleur's memoir *Land of a Thousand Sorrows*.

p. 110 To quote Lord Durham....
John George Lambton Durham, *Lord Durham's Report on the Affairs of British North America*, 307.

p. 111 As Robert Baldwin said....
Quoted in *Kingston Herald*, 14 May 1844.

p. 113 In the Atlantic colonies, similar hard-fought battles....
This section draws on Phillip Buckner and John Reid's *The Atlantic Region to Confederation*, 263–307.

p. 115 The Tory press fed the mood of crisis....
Stephen Leacock, *Baldwin, LaFontaine and Hincks*, 343–4.

p. 115–16 As John Ralston Saul noted....
John Saul Ralston, "2000 LaFontaine Baldwin Lecture," in *Dialogue on Democracy in Canada*, ed. Rudyard Griffiths, 8.

p. 118 Stephen Leacock describes this period....
Stephen Leacock, *Baldwin, LaFontaine and Hincks*, 306.

6 | CANADA FOUND — AND LOST

p. 125 As historian Robert Bothwell describes it....
Robert Bothwell, *Canada since 1945*, 58.

p. 126 In the words of historian William Kilbourn....
William Kilbourn, "The 1950s," in *The Canadians, 1867–1967*, eds. J.M.S. Careless and R. Craig Brown, 316.

p. 127 Tommy Douglas had established....
Quoted in "House of Assembly—Member's Statement," 2 December 2004, http://www.nl.ndp.ca (accessed 12 September 2008).

p. 129 As Walter Harris, a St. Laurent finance minister....
Quoted in J. W. Pickersgill, *My Years with Louis St. Laurent*, 310.

p. 132 In Martin's words....
Paul Martin, "Citizenship and the People's World," in *Belonging*, ed. William Kaplan, 69–70.

p. 133 Norman Robertson commented at the time....
Quoted in J.L. Granatstein, *A Man of Influence*, 236.

p. 135 Pearson won the Nobel Peace Prize....
Lester B. Pearson, *Mike*, 274.

p. 137 In terms of domestic policy....
Robert Fulford, "Anti-Americanism, Bred in the Bone," *National Post*, 17 November 2005, A27.

p. 142 Historian Jack Granatstein sums up....

J.L. Granatstein, *Yankee Go Home?*, 286.

p. 145 As George Grant and others have observed....

"The French Canadians had entered Confederation not to protect the
rights of the individual but the rights of a nation. They did not want
to be swallowed up by that sea which Henri Bourassa had called
'l'américanisme-saxonisant.'" George Grant, *Lament for a Nation*, 22.

7 | OUR THIRD IMAGINING

p. 154 In the words of Desmond Morton....

Desmond Morton, "Divided Loyalties? Divided Country?," in *Belonging*,
ed. William Kaplan, 59–60.

p. 155 And, as political scientist Thomas Homer-Dixon....

Thomas Homer-Dixon, "Prepare Today for Tomorrow's Breakdown,"
Globe and Mail, 14 May 2007, A17.

p. 160 In addition to the expectation....

John Chant, "The Passport Package: Rethinking the Citizenship Benefits of
Non-Resident Canadians," *C.D. Howe Institute Backgrounder*, No. 99 (2006), 5–6.

p. 162 The fact that one in three immigrant families....

Statistics Canada, *Earnings and Income of Canadians Over the Last Quarter
Century, 2006 Census* (Ottawa: Statistics Canada, 2006), No. 97–563–XIE, 44.

p. 165 As political scientist Henry Milner....

Henry Milner, *Civic Literacy*, 25.

p. 167 Four out of five....

Dominion Institute, "Remembrance Day Survey," 9 November 2007,
http://www.dominion.ca/polling.htm (accessed 12 September 2008).

p. 168 The statistics speak for themselves....

Janice Aurini and Scott Davies, "Choice without Markets: Homeschooling
in the Context of Private Education," *British Journal of Sociology of Education*,
24:4 (2005), 461.

p. 168 For example, approximately 7 percent....

Jasmin Zine, "Safe Havens or Religious 'Ghettos'?: Narratives of Islamic
Schooling in Canada," *Race, Ethnicity and Education*, 24:4 (2007), 73.

p. 168 Studies undertaken in the last decade....

Claudia Hepburn and William Robson, *Learning from Success: What
Americans Can Learn from School Choice in Canada* (Vancouver: Fraser
Institute, 2002), 29.

8 | A CONFESSION AND A PROPOSAL

p. 175 Yes, despite my conviction....

Statistics Canada reports that there are 850,000 dual citizens in Canada (see Statistics Canada, 2006 *Census*, No. 97–557–XCB2006004). It is important to note that this figure does not encompass the estimated 1.7 million Canadian citizens who live abroad permanently (see Kenny Zhang, "Recognizing the Canadian Diaspora," *Canada Asia Commentary*, No. 41 [March 2006], www.asiapacific.ca). Statistics Canada's 850,000 dual citizens living in

Canada are also far fewer than the approximately 2.5 million Canadian citizens, eighteen years of age or older, who told Ipsos Reid in 2007 that they held a second citizenship (see Dominion Institute, "Canadian Born Dual Citizens," 30 September 2007, http://www.dominion.ca/polling.htm. [accessed 12 September 2008]).

p. 176 Nonetheless, I was surprised to learn....

Dominion Institute, "Canadian Born Dual Citizens," 30 September 2007, http://www.dominion.ca/polling.htm (accessed 12 September 2008).

| SELECTED BIBLIOGRAPHY

Adams, Michael, with Amy Langstaff. *Unlikely Utopia: The Surprising Triumph of Canadian Pluralism*. Toronto: Viking Canada, 2007.

Ajzenstat, Janet, and William Gairdner, eds. *Canada's Founding Debates*. Toronto: Stoddart, 1999.

Ajzenstat, Janet, and Peter J. Smith, eds. *Canada's Origins: Liberal, Tory, or Republican*. Ottawa: Carleton University Press, 1995.

Anderson, Charles D. *Bluebloods and Rednecks: Discord and Rebellion in the 1830s*. Burnstown: The General Store Publishing House, 1996.

Banting, Keith, Thomas Courchene, and Leslie Seidle, eds. *Belonging?: Diversity, Recognition and Shared Citizenship in Canada*. Montreal: IRPP, 2007.

Bissoondath, Neil. *Selling Illusions: The Cult of Multiculturalism in Canada*. Toronto: Penguin, 1994.

Bothwell, Robert, Ian Drummond, and John English. *Canada since 1945: Power, Politics and Provincialism*. Toronto: University of Toronto Press, 1981.

Bothwell, Robert, and J.L. Granatstein. *Our Century: The Canadian Journey*. Toronto: McArthur, 2000.

Broadbent, Alan. *Urban Nation: Why We Need to Give Power back to the Cities to Make Canada Strong*. Toronto: HarperCollins, 2008.

Buckner, Phillip A., and John G. Reid, eds. *The Atlantic Region to Confederation: A History*. Toronto: University of Toronto Press, 1994.

Byers, Michael. *Intent for a Nation: What Is Canada For?* Vancouver: Douglas & McIntyre, 2007.

Careless, J.M.S., and R. Craig Brown, eds. *The Canadians, 1867–1967*. Toronto: Macmillan, 1967.

Cohen, Andrew. *While Canada Slept: How We Lost Our Place in the World*. Toronto: McClelland & Stewart, 2003.

———. *The Unfinished Canadian: The People We Are*. Toronto: McClelland & Stewart, 2007.

Durham, John George Lambton. *Lord Durham's Report on the Affairs of British North America*. Oxford: Clarendon Press, 1912.

Godfrey, John, and Rob McLean. *The Canada We Want" Competing Visions for the New Millenium*. Toronto: Stoddart, 1999.

Granatstein, J.L. *A Man of Influence: Norman A. Robertson and Canadian Statecraft, 1929–68*. Montreal: Deneau Publishers, 1981.

———. *Yankee Go Home?: Canadians and Anti-Americanism*. Toronto: HarperCollins, 1996.

———. *Who Killed Canadian History?* Toronto: Harper Perennial, 2007.

———. *Whose War Is It?: How Canada Can Survive in the Post-9/11 World*. Toronto: HarperCollins, 2007.

Granatstein, J.L., M. A. Irving, T. W. Acheson, D. J. Bercuson, R. C. Brown, and H. B. Neatby, eds. *Nation: Canada Since Confederation*. 3rd ed. Toronto: McGraw-Hill Ryerson, 1990.

Grant, George. *Lament for a Nation: The Defeat of Canadian Nationalism*. 40th Anniversary Edition. Montreal: McGill-Queen's University Press, 2005.

Gregg, Allan R. *The Big Picture: What Canadians Think about Almost Everything*. Toronto: Macfarlane Walter & Ross, 1990.

Greer, Allan. *The Patriots and the People: The Rebellion of 1837 in Rural Lower Canada*. Toronto: University of Toronto Press, 1993.

Griffiths, Rudyard, ed. *Great Questions of Canada*. Toronto: Stoddart, 2000.

——— ed. *Story of a Nation: Defining Moments in Our History*. Toronto: Doubleday Canada, 2001.

——— ed. *Passages: Welcome Home to Canada*. Toronto: Doubleday Canada, 2002.

——— ed. *Our Story: Aboriginal Voices on Canada's Past*. Toronto: Doubleday Canada, 2004.

——— ed. *Dialogue on Democracy in Canada: The LaFontaine-Baldwin Lectures, 2000–2005*. Toronto: Penguin, 2006.

———. "Ambition and Loyalty: The Making of John A. Macdonald and Confederation," *Historic Kingston*, Vol. 54 (2006), 2-17.

———— ed. *Canada in 2020: Twenty Leading Voices Imagine Canada's Future.* Toronto: Key Porter Books, 2008.

———— ed. *American Myths: What Canadians Think They Know About The United States.* Toronto: Key Porter Books, 2008.

———— ed. *101 Things Canadians Should Know About Canada.* Toronto: Key Porter Books, 2008.

Gruending, Dennis, ed. *Great Canadian Speeches.* Markham: Fitzhenry & Whiteside, 2004.

Gwyn, Richard. *Nationalism Without Walls: The Unbearable Lightness of Being Canadian.* Toronto: McClelland & Stewart, 1995.

————. *Rediscovering Our Citizenship.* Toronto: Dominion Institute, 1997.

————. "The World's First Anti-Americans: Canada as the Canary in the Global Mine." *Munk Center Distinguished Lecture Series.* Toronto: Munk Center for International Studies, 2008.

Haskayne, Dick, with Paul Grescoe. *Northern Tigers: Building Ethical Canadian Corporate Champions.* Toronto: Key Porter Books, 2007.

Hirsch, E.D. *The Schools We Need and Why We Don't Have Them.* New York: Doubleday, 1996.

Homer-Dixon, Thomas. *The Ingenuity Gap: How We Can Solve the Problems of the Future.* London: Jonathan Cape, 2000.

Huntington, Samuel P. *Who Are We?: The Challenges to America's National Identity.* New York: Simon & Schuster, 2004.

Ibbitson, John. *The Polite Revolution: Perfecting the Canadian Dream.* Toronto: McClelland & Stewart, 2005.

Ignatieff, Michael. *Rights Revolution.* 2nd Edition. Toronto: House of Anansi Press, 2007.

Iyer, Pico. *The Global Soul: Jet Lag, Shopping Malls, and the Search for Home.* Toronto: Knopf, 2001.

Kaplan, William, ed. *Belonging: The Meaning and Future of Canadian Citizenship.* Montreal and Kingston: McGill-Queen's University Press, 1993.

Lasch, Christopher. *The True and Only Heaven: Progress and Its Critics.* New York: Norton, 1991.

————. *The Revolt of the Elites and the Betrayal of Democracy.* New York: Norton, 1995.

Latimer, Jon. *1812: War with America.* Cambridge: Belknap Press of Harvard University Press, 2007.

Leacock, Stephen. *Baldwin, LaFontaine and Hincks: Responsible Government.* Toronto: University of Toronto, 1965.

Lepailleur, Francois-Maurice. *Land of a Thousand Sorrows: The Australian Prison Journal, 1840–1842, of the Exiled Canadian Patriote, Francois-Maurice Lepailleur.* Trans. and ed. F. Murray Greenwood. Vancouver: University of British Columbia, 1980.

Luciani, Patrick, and Rudyard Griffiths, eds. *American Power: Potential and Limits in the Twenty-first Century.* Toronto: Key Porter Books, 2007.

Mills, David. *The Idea of Loyalty in Upper Canada, 1784–1850.* Kingston: McGill-Queen's University Press, 1988.

Milner, Henry. *Civic Literacy: How Informed Citizens Make Democracy Work.* Hanover: University Press of New England, 2002.

Monbiot, George. *Heat: How to Stop the Planet from Burning.* Toronto: Doubleday Canada, 2006.

Monet, Jacques. *The Last Cannon Shot: A Study of French Canadian Nationalism, 1837–1850.* Toronto: University of Toronto Press, 1969.

Moore, Christopher. *1867: How the Fathers Made a Deal.* Toronto: McClelland & Stewart, 1997.

Morton, W.L. *The Canadian Identity.* Toronto: University of Toronto Press, 1972.

Moskos, Charles C. *A Call to Civic Service: National Service for Country and Community.* New York: Free Press, 1988.

Newman, Peter C. *The Canadian Revolution, 1985–1995: from Deference to Defiance.* Toronto: Viking, 1995.

———. *Defining Moments: Dispatches from an Unfinished Revolution.* Toronto: Viking, 1997.

Pachauri, R.K., and A. Reisinger. *Climate Change 2007: Synthesis Report.* Geneva: IPCC, 2007.

Pearson, Lester B. *Mike: The Memoirs of the Right Honourable Lester B. Pearson.* Vol. 2, 1948–1957. University of Toronto Press, 1972.

Pickersgill, J.W. *My Years with Louis St. Laurent: A Political Memoir.* Toronto: University of Toronto Press, 1975.

Powe, B.W. *Towards a Canada of Light.* Toronto: Thomas Allen Publishers, 2006.

Pratte, André, ed. *Reconquering Canada: Quebec Federalists Speak Up for Change.* Vancouver: Douglas & McIntyre, 2008.

Resnick, Philip. *Thinking English Canada.* Don Mills: Stoddart, 1994.

———. *The European Roots of Canadian Identity.* Peterborough: Broadview Press, 2005.

Richler, Noah. *This Is My Country, What's Yours?: A Literary Atlas of Canada.* Toronto, McClelland & Stewart, 2006.

Sandel, Michael J. *Democracy's Discontent: America in Search for a Public Philosophy.* Cambridge: Belknap Press of Harvard University Press, 1996.

———. *Public Philosophy: Essays on Morality in Politics.* Cambridge: Harvard University Press, 2005.

Sandwell, Ruth W. *To the Past: History Education, Public Memory, and Citizenship in Canada.* Toronto: University of Toronto Press, 2006.

Saul, John Ralston. *Reflections of A Siamese Twin: Canada at the End of the Twentieth Century.* Toronto: Viking, 1997.

———. *The Collapse of Globalism and the Reinvention of the World.* Toronto: Viking Canada, 2005.

———. *Joseph Howe and the Battle for Freedom of Speech.* Kentville: Gaspereau Press, 2006.

———. *A Fair Country: Telling Truths about Canada.* Toronto: Viking Canada, 2008.

Stoffman, Daniel. *Who Gets In: What's Wrong with Canada's Immigration Program and How to Fix It.* Toronto: Macfarlane Walter & Ross, 2002.

Strachan, John. *A Discourse on the Character of King George the Third: Addressed to the Inhabitants of British America.* Montreal: Nahum Mower, 1810.

Tainter, Joseph A. *The Collapse of Complex Societies.* Cambridge and New York: Cambridge University Press, 1988.

Taylor, Charles. *The Malaise of Modernity.* Toronto: House of Anansi Press, 1991.

———. *Hegel and Modern Society.* Cambridge: Cambridge University Press, 1979.

Vance, Jonathan F. W. *Building Canada: People and Projects that Shaped the Nation.* Toronto: Penguin Canada, 2006.

| INDEX